Knitting Patterns and Essays with Robust Flavor

COFFEEHOUSE
Knits

Interweave

Published by Interweave
Books, an imprint of F+W
Media, Inc., 10151 Carver
Road, Suite 300, Blue Ash,
Ohio 45242. First Edition.

www.fwcommunity.com

www.interweave.com

23 22 21 20 19   5 4 3 2 1

SRN: 19KN02

ISBN13: 978-1-63250-659-7

EDITORIAL DIRECTOR
Kerry Bogert

CONTENT EDITOR
Erica Smith

TECHNICAL EDITOR
Susan Moskwa

ART DIRECTOR
Ashlee Wadeson

COVER & INTERIOR
DESIGNER Pamela Norman

ILLUSTRATOR
Ann Swanson

PHOTOGRAPHY
Caleb Young

Special thanks to Toast Coffee & Wine Bar Windsor, CO

CONTENTS

INTRODUCTION

IF YOU'VE BEEN KNITTING for any length of time, there's no doubt you've formed a bit of a ritual when it comes to your time spent stitching. For me, it's shuffling downstairs in the early morning hours before the rest of the house wakes. I brew some coffee (hazelnut cream, please, no need for extra sugar), pour a steaming hot cup, and sit in my favorite corner of the couch knitting until it's time to get the kids off to school. I find myself wishing I could linger there all day, but sooner or later work calls. Luckily, my work is creating craft books like the one you're reading now, or the urge to pour another cup would be too difficult to resist.

I find a habit has developed around my knitting outside the house as well. When my knitting friends gather, it's almost always in a coffee shop. Before heading out the door to the coffeehouse, a few things must happen. First, I need to wear my latest finished project. Surely I was working on it the last time I saw everyone and they'd need to see how it turned out. Then, knitting bag packing. I've long since thrown out the idea that I should only bring a travel-friendly project with me for gatherings. While I do try to bring something I won't mess up during distracted moments of chit-chatting, I'm not afraid to bring a sweater if that's what I'm feeling most inspired to work on. Last, a spare skein or two. If I've made a recent stash enhancement, I love to share what I've found with friends. If I've recently culled a few skeins, I bring them knowing they'll find a good home by the end of the visit.

These two simple acts, my quiet morning knitting and time spent with my knitting friends, are at the heart of the inspiration for the projects featured in this book. I know I'm not alone in either of these doings. Though our routines and caffeine tolerance may differ, I'm sure you know the comfort and connection these actions bring. In that vein, you'll find projects to keep you entertained during solitary times, alongside ones you could easily knit while talking with friends. Don't be afraid to stop and sip your drink of choice; it will be easy to pick up where you left off. You'll also discover beautiful yarns that will be buttery in your hands and others you'll jump to show your companions. All the while, the combination of design and fiber has the focus of being classic and wearable, so you'll love wearing these on outings just as much as knitting them.

And what's better over coffee than engaging conversation? So along with patterns, you'll find essays from knitters just like you. Each has a unique perspective on their relationship with knitting and what being a part of this great community has provided them. Consider this book an invitation. Pour yourself a cuppa, grab your needles and yarn, pull up a chair, and join us. We're so very glad you're here.

Kerry Bogert — Knitter and Editorial Director, Books

PATTERNS

| | | | | | | | | | | | | | | | | | | | | | | |

I ADMIT, I'M A JAVA-HOLIC, and I've had more than my share of nonfat cappuccinos with the coffee gals, but on rare occasions I've been known to break routine for a secret indulgence reminiscent of my childhood: hot chocolate. Not just your typical steaming cup of cocoa, but one topped-to-overflowing with smushy-soft marshmallows (smush-mallows, as I called them), like the ones I drank over stories and laughs with the important gals of my youth—my sister, mom, and grandma—the same women who taught me to knit on now-vintage needles in rainbow colors. I got good advice from them that I'll pass on to you: don't abandon your knitting too long, don't stop gathering with your pals to laugh and chat, and please don't forget to treat yourself to an occasional hot cocoa overflowing with smush-mallows, because you're worth it.

Amy Rollis

LATTE SWIRL
Sweater

This sweater is knit seamlessly from the top down. The patterning around the yoke is designed to be reminiscent of those fancy swirls baristas make with milk foam atop espresso beverages. The combination of lace and cables makes these swirls pop in an unusual and organic fashion. — **AMY GUNDERSON**

FINISHED SIZE

About 32 (36, 40, 44, 48, 52, 56, 60)" (81.5 [91.5, 101.5, 112, 122, 132, 142, 152.5] cm) bust circumference.

Garment shown measures 36" (91.5 cm), modeled with 2" (2.5 cm) of ease.

YARN

DK weight (#3 light).

Shown here: Fibra Natura Dona (100% extrafine superwash Merino wool; 126 yd [115 m]/1¾ oz [50 g]): #117 blackberry, 9 (10, 11, 12, 13, 15, 16, 17) balls.

NEEDLES

Size U.S. 4 (3.5 mm): 16" (40 cm) circular (cir), set of double-pointed (dpn).

Size U.S. 6 (4 mm): 32" (80 cm) cir, set of dpn.

Adjust needle size if necessary to obtain the correct gauge.

NOTIONS

Stitch markers (m); cable needle (cn); stitch holders or waste yarn; tapestry needle.

GAUGE

20 sts and 28 rnds = 4" (10 cm) in Stockinette st with larger needle after blocking.

NOTES

— The yoke increases are worked into the charted pattern. After the chart is completed, increases continue in raglan fashion.

— In the yoke section, when there are too many stitches to fit comfortably on the 16" (40 cm) circular needle, switch to longer needle.

Instructions

YOKE

With smaller needle, CO 90 (100, 100, 110, 110, 120, 120, 130) sts. Pm and join for working in the round, being careful not to twist.

Knit 2 rnds.

Switch to larger needle.

Next rnd: *K10, pm; rep from * to end.

Work Rnds 1–38 of Yoke Chart —216 (240, 240, 264, 264, 288, 288, 312) sts. Remov e all markers except beg-of-rnd m.

ESTABLISH RAGLAN INCREASES

Set-up rnd: K22 (24, 23, 24, 23, 25, 24, 25), pm, knit across 64 (72, 74, 84, 86, 94, 96, 106) front sts, pm, knit across 44 (48, 46, 48, 46, 50, 48, 50) left sleeve sts, pm, knit across 64 (72, 74, 84, 86, 94, 96, 106) back sts, pm, k22 (24, 23, 24, 23, 25, 24, 25), remove beg-of-rnd m, knit to next m. This next m is the new beg of rnd.

Inc rnd: *Sl m, k1, M1L, knit to 1 st before m, M1R, k1; rep from * 3 more times —8 sts inc'd.

Rep Inc rnd every 4 (4, 2, 2, 2, 2, 2) rnds 3 (3, 5, 2, 8, 7, 14, 11) more times, then rep Inc rnd every - (- , 4, 4, 4, 4, - , 4) rnds - (- , 2, 4, 2, 3, - , 2) times —248 (272, 304, 320, 352, 376, 408, 424) sts; 72 (80, 90, 98, 108, 116, 126, 134) sts each front and back, 52 (56, 62, 62, 68, 72, 78, 78) sts each sleeve.

Work even in St st until yoke measures 8 (8½, 9, 9½, 10, 10¼, 10½, 10¾)" (20.5 [21.5, 23, 24, 25.5, 26, 26.5, 27.5] cm).

YOKE CHART

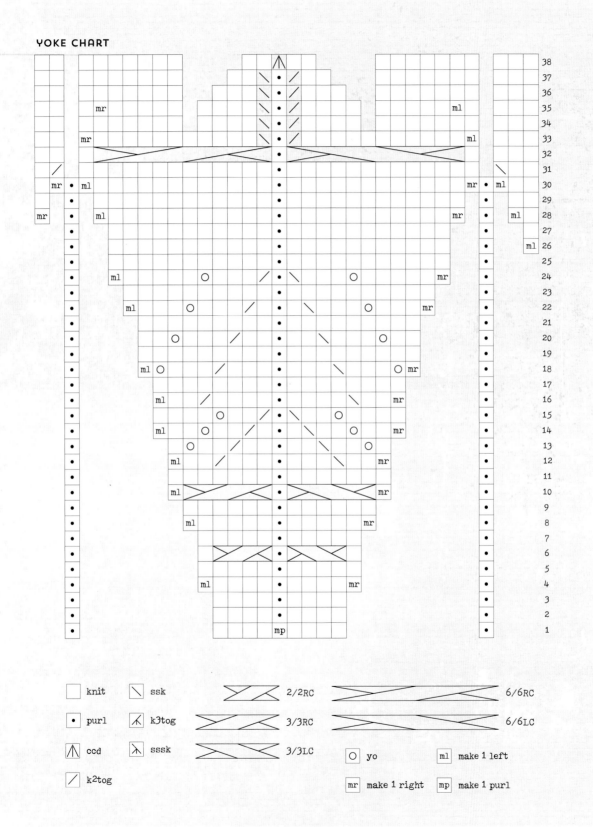

knit	ssk	2/2RC
purl	k3tog	3/3RC
ccd	sssk	3/3LC
k2tog		

6/6RC
6/6LC
yo — make 1 left
mr — make 1 right   mp — make 1 purl

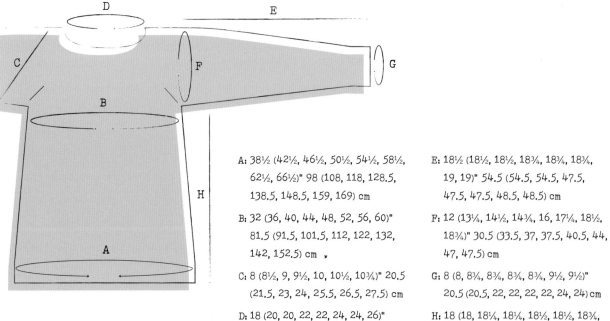

A: 38½ (42½, 46½, 50½, 54½, 58½, 62½, 66½)" 98 (108, 118, 128.5, 138.5, 148.5, 159, 169) cm

B: 32 (36, 40, 44, 48, 52, 56, 60)" 81.5 (91.5, 101.5, 112, 122, 132, 142, 152.5) cm ↘

C: 8 (8½, 9, 9½, 10, 10½, 10¾)" 20.5 (21.5, 23, 24, 25.5, 26.5, 27.5) cm

D: 18 (20, 20, 22, 22, 24, 24, 26)" 45.5 (51, 51, 56, 56, 61, 61, 66) cm

E: 18½ (18½, 18½, 18¾, 18¾, 18¾, 19, 19)" 54.5 (54.5, 54.5, 47.5, 47.5, 47.5, 48.5, 48.5) cm

F: 12 (13¼, 14½, 14¾, 16, 17¼, 18½, 18¾)" 30.5 (33.5, 37, 37.5, 40.5, 44, 47, 47.5) cm

G: 8 (8, 8¾, 8¾, 8¾, 8¾, 9½, 9½)" 20.5 (20.5, 22, 22, 22, 22, 24, 24) cm

H: 18 (18, 18¼, 18¼, 18½, 18½, 18¾, 18¾)" 45.5 (45.5, 46.5, 47, 47) cm

SEPARATE BODY AND SLEEVES

Rnd 1: Remove beg-of-rnd m, knit across 72 (80, 90, 98, 108, 116, 126, 134) front sts, remove m, place next 52 (56, 62, 62, 68, 72, 78, 78) sleeve sts on holder or waste yarn, remove m, CO 4 (5, 5, 6, 6, 7, 7, 8) sts, pm for side, CO 4 (5, 5, 6, 6, 7, 7, 8) sts, knit across 72 (80, 90, 98, 108, 116, 126, 134) back sts, remove m, place next 52 (56, 62, 62, 68, 72, 78, 78) sleeve sts on holder or waste yarn, remove m, CO 4 (5, 5, 6, 6, 7, 7, 8) sts, pm for side and new beg of rnd, CO 4 (5, 5, 6, 6, 7, 7, 8) sts—160 (180, 200, 220, 240, 260, 280, 300) sts rem for body.

Work even in St st until piece measures 1" (2.5 cm) from separation.

Inc rnd: *K1, M1L, knit to 1 st before m, M1R, k1; rep from * 1 more time—4 sts inc'd.

Rep Inc rnd every 12 rnds 7 more times—192 (212, 232, 252, 272, 292, 312, 332) sts.

Work even in St st until piece measures 16¼ (16¼, 16½, 16½, 16¾, 16¾, 17, 17)" (41.5 [41.5, 42, 42, 42.5, 42.5, 43, 43] cm).

HEM

Switch to smaller needle.

Rnds 1–10: *K2, p2; rep from * to end.

Switch to larger needle.
Knit 2 rnds. BO all sts.

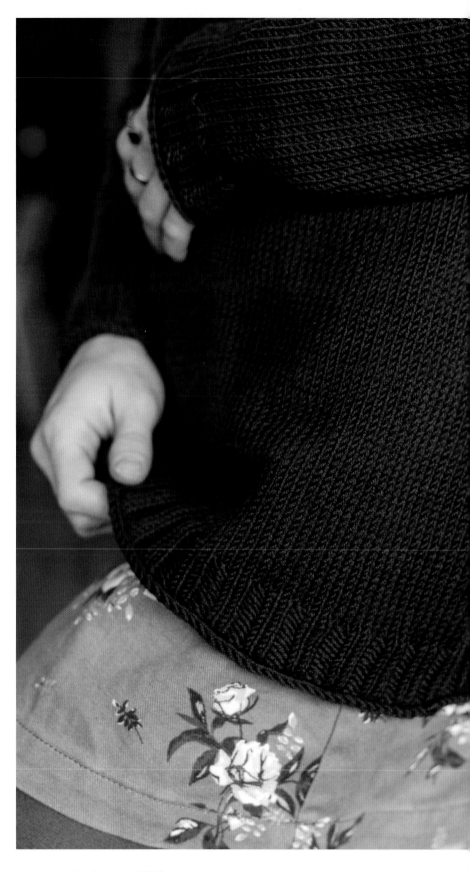

SLEEVES (MAKE 2)

With larger needle, return 52 (56, 62, 62, 68, 72, 78, 78) sleeve sts to dpn and distribute evenly.

Rnd 1: Beg at center of underarm CO, pick up and knit 4 (5, 5, 6, 6, 7, 7, 8) sts, knit across sleeve sts, pick up and knit 4 (5, 5, 6, 6, 7, 7, 8) sts from other side of underarm CO —60 (66, 72, 74, 80, 86, 92, 94) sts. Pm and join to work in the rnd.

Work even in St st until sleeve measures 3" (7.5 cm).

Dec rnd: K2tog, knit to last 3 sts, ssk, k1—2 sts dec'd.

Rep Dec rnd every 10 (8, 8, 8, 6, 6, 6) rnds 6 (7, 4, 2, 11, 5, 4, 2) more times, then rep Dec rnd every 8 (6, 6, 6, 4, 4, 4, 4) rnds 3 (5, 9, 12, 6, 15, 17, 20) times —40 (40, 44, 44, 44, 44, 48, 48) sts.

Work even in St st until sleeve measures 17 (17, 17, 17¼, 17¼, 17¼, 17½, 17½)" (43 [43, 43, 44, 44, 44, 44.5, 44.5] cm).

CUFF

Switch to smaller needle.

Rnds 1–10: *K2, p2; rep from * to end.

Switch to larger needle. Knit 2 rnds. BO all sts.

FINISHING

Sew underarm seams. Weave in ends. Block piece to finished measurements.

Fudge Swirls SCARF

I have a huge weakness for something sweet alongside my coffee—
especially fudge packaged in pretty twists of shiny paper.
The cable pattern used in this scarf brings these beauties to
mind! The scarf is worked flat from end to end, and you have
the option to finish it with a deep fringe. The cable pattern is
engaging but straightforward, so you can concentrate on coffee
and chatting, not the pattern. — **SUE GLEAVE**

FINISHED SIZE
About 72" (183 cm)
long without fringe and
12" (30.5 cm) wide.

YARN
Aran weight (#4 medium).

Shown here: Native Yarns
Rendlesham (100%
Bluefaced Leicester wool;
175 yd [160 m]/3½ oz
[100 g]): silva, 5 skeins.

NEEDLES
Size U.S. 6 (4 mm).

*Adjust needle size if
necessary to obtain
the correct gauge.*

NOTIONS
2 cable needles (cn); tapestry
needle; scissors (for fringe).

GAUGE
26 sts and 28 rows = 4"
(10 cm) in Cable Stitch
patt after blocking.

NOTE
— The cable stitches can
be worked as per the
instructions; this is the
purist's way and matches
up with standard charting
symbols. There's also an
alternative way to work these
cables, which is swifter to
knit and less fiddly. This is
given in the Stitch Guide.
Consider trying them both
out in a swatch and deciding
which method you like
best. The appearance of
the cables is identical when
viewed from the front of the
scarf. Personally, I prefer the
back of the "cheat" version
as it has a smoother, less
bobbly appearance. The
choice, as they say, is yours!

2/2/2RPC: Sl 4 sts to cn and hold in back, k2 from left needle, [p2, k2] from cn.

2/2/2LPC: Sl 2 sts to cn and hold in front, [k2, p2] from left needle, k2 from cn.

Cable Stitch pattern, worked flat over 60 stitches

Row 1: [K2, p2] 8 times, 2/2/2 RPC, p2, [k2, p2] 5 times.

Row 2 and all WS rows: Knit all knit sts and purl all purl sts.

Row 3: [K2, p2] 7 times, 2/2/2RPC, p2, [k2, p2] 6 times.

Row 5: [K2, p2] 6 times, 2/2/2RPC, p2, 2/2/2RPC, p2, [k2, p2] 5 times.

Row 7: [K2, p2] 5 times, 2/2/2RPC, p2, 2/2/2RPC, p2, [k2, p2] 6 times.

Row 9: Rep Row 5.

Row 11: Rep Row 7.

Row 13: Rep Row 5.

Row 15: Rep Row 7.

Row 17: [K2, p2] 6 times, 2/2/2RPC, p2, [k2, p2] 7 times.

Row 19: [K2, p2] 5 times, 2/2/2RPC, p2, [k2, p2] 8 times.

Row 21: 2/2/2LPC, p2, [k2, p2] 8 times, 2/2/2LPC, p2, [k2, p2] 3 times.

Row 23: K2, p2, 2/2/2LPC, p2, [k2, p2] 8 times, 2/2/2LPC, p2, [k2, p2] twice.

Row 25: [2/2/2LPC, p2] twice, [k2, p2] 6 times, [2/2/2LPC, p2] twice, k2, p2.

Row 27: K2, p2, [2/2/2LPC, p2] twice, [k2, p2] 6 times, [2/2/2LPC, p2] twice.

Row 29: Rep Row 25.

Row 31: Rep Row 27.

Row 33: Rep Row 25.

Row 35: Rep Row 27.

Row 37: [K2, p2] twice, 2/2/2LPC, p2, [k2, p2] 8 times, 2/2/2LPC, p2, k2, p2.

Row 39: [K2, p2] 3 times, 2/2/2LPC, p2, [k2, p2] 8 times, 2/2/2LPC, p2.

Instructions

CO 70 sts.

Row 1: K4, p2, *k2, p2; rep from * to last 4 sts, k4.

Row 2: K4, *k2, p2; rep from * to last 6 sts, k6.

Row 3 and all RS rows: K4, p2, work Cable Stitch patt (see Stitch Guide, above, or chart on page 21) to last 4 sts, k4.

Row 4 and all WS rows: K4, work Cable Stitch patt to last 6 sts, k6.

Repeat Rows 3 and 4 until you've worked 11½ reps of Cable Stitch patt, ending after Row 20—462 total rows worked.

Row 463: K4, p2, *k2, p2; rep from * to last 4 sts, k4.

Row 464: BO in rib patt.

FINISHING

Weave in ends and cut yarn for fringe. I suggest placing the fringe on each ridge of the rib. I used 6 strands cut to 14" (35.5 cm) doubled for each tassel and tied, then trimmed to a length of 6" (15 cm).

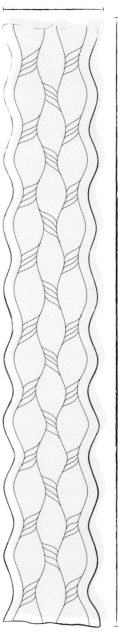

12" (30.5 cm)

72"
(183 cm)

CABLE STITCH CHART

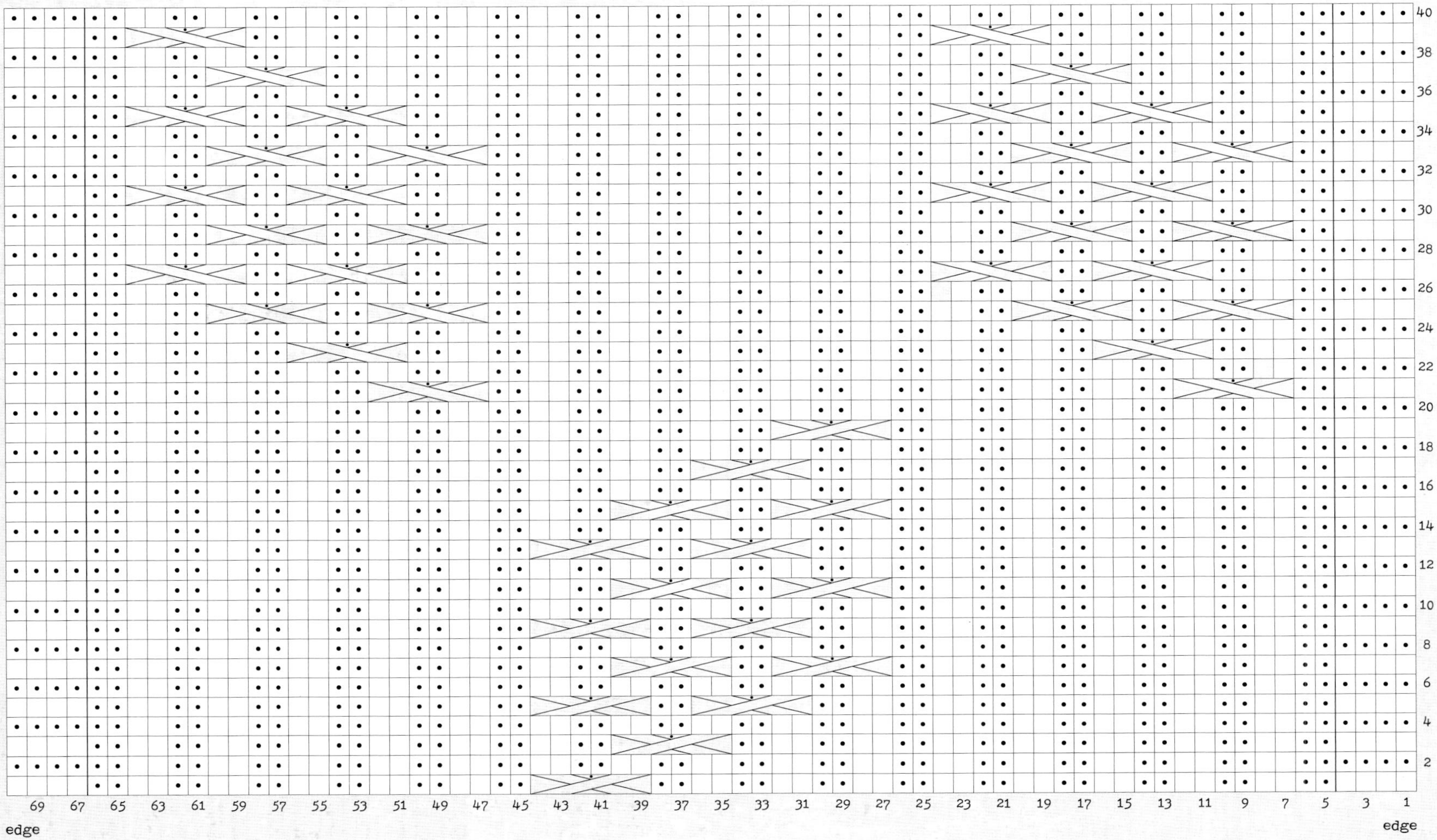

knit on RS, purl on WS

• purl on RS, knit on WS

2/2/2LPC

2/2/2RPC

Chai Latte COWL

The Chai Latte Cowl is a perfect take-along project, and with only a two-row repeat, it is easy to knit while carrying on a conversation. The cowl begins with a 2×1 ribbing, transitioning into a Broken Rib pattern. As you work the cowl, a faux cable created by yarnovers and decreases creates a Stockinette section that widens as the Broken Rib pattern decreases, highlighting the contrast of the two stitch patterns, with the top border worked in a complementary 2×1 ribbing. — **LORI WAGNER**

FINISHED SIZE
About 26½" (67.5 cm) circumference, and 17½" (44.5 cm) tall.

YARN
Worsted weight (#4 medium).

Shown here: Malabrigo Rios (100% superwash Merino wool; 210 yd [192 m]/3½ oz [100 g]): #131 sand bank, 2 balls.

NEEDLES
Size U.S. 7 (4.5 mm): 16" (40 cm) circular (cir).

Adjust needle size if necessary to obtain the correct gauge.

NOTIONS
3 stitch markers (m), 1 distinctive to mark beg of rnd; tapestry needle.

GAUGE
18 sts and 28 rnds = 4" (10 cm) in Stockinette st after blocking.

18 sts and 30 rnds = 4" (10 cm) in Broken Rib patt after blocking.

NOTE
— Two stitch markers are used in the pattern to easily identify where to decrease. Before working the decrease, the stitch marker will be moved one stitch to the right or left on every other row. As you work the cowl, you might find it easy to see where the decreases occur and may want to remove these markers.

Broken Rib pattern

Rnd 1: Knit.

Rnd 2: *K2, p1; repeat from * to end.

Repeat Rnds 1 and 2 for pattern.

Instructions

CO 120 sts using the long-tail cast-on. Pm and join for working in the round, being careful not to twist.

BOTTOM BORDER

Rnd 1: K1, *p1, k2; rep from * to 2 sts before end, p1, k1.

Work Rnd 1 three more times.

BODY OF COWL

Rnd 1: K1, yo, k1, ssk, pm, knit to 4 sts before end, pm, k2tog, k1, yo, k1.

Rnd 2: K4, sl m, *p1, k2; rep from * to 1 st before m, p1, sl m, k4.

Rnd 3: K2, yo, k1, sl1, remove m, move sl st back to left needle, ssk, pm, knit to 1 st before m, sl1, remove m, move sl st back to left needle, pm, k2tog, k1, yo, k2.

Rnd 4: K5, sl m, *k2, p1; repeat from * to 2 sts before m, k2, sl m, knit to end.

Rnd 5: Knit to 2 sts before m, yo, k1, sl1, remove m, move sl st back to left needle, ssk, pm, knit to 1 st before m, sl1, remove m, move sl st back to left needle, pm, k2tog, k1, yo, knit to end.

Rnd 6: Knit to m, sl m, k1, *p1, k2; repeat from * to 2 sts before m, p1, k1, sl m, knit to end.

Rnd 7: Rep Rnd 5.

Rnd 8: Knit to m, sl m, *p1, k2; repeat from * to 1 st before m, p1, sl m, knit to end.

Rnd 9: Rep Rnd 5.

Rnd 10: Knit to m, sl m, *k2, p1; repeat from * to 2 sts before m, k2, sl m, knit to end.

Repeat Rnds 5–10 sixteen more times.

Repeat Rnds 5–9 once more.

Rnd 112: Knit to end.

Rnd 113: Knit to 2 sts before m, yo, k1, sl1, remove m, move sl st back to left needle, ssk, pm, sl1, remove m, move sl st back to left needle, k2tog, k1, yo, knit to end.

Rnd 114: Knit to end.

Rnd 115: Knit to 2 sts before m, yo, ssk, remove m, k2tog, yo, knit to end.

Rnd 116: Knit to end.

TOP BORDER

Work as for Bottom Border.

FINISHING

BO in pattern. Cut yarn, leaving a 6" (15 cm) tail, and pull through remaining st. Weave in ends and block to finished measurements.

GINGERSNAP *Pullover*

This classic pullover is topped with a wide, flattering neck and an interesting hem, both trimmed with I-cord. Garter-stitch columns create depth of texture and achieve a strong vertical dynamic without sacrificing drape. The garter stitch behaves beautifully with a bateau neckline because it is not inclined to curl. Made with simple knits and purls, it makes for perfect coffeehouse knitting. — **CHERYL TOY**

FINISHED SIZE

About 36 (40, 43½, 47, 52½, 56)" (91.5 [101.5, 110.5, 119.5, 133.5, 142] cm) bust circumference.

Designed to have about 3–4" (7.5–10 cm) of positive ease.

Garment shown measures 40" (101.5 cm), modeled with 6" (15 cm) of ease.

YARN

Sportweight (#2 fine).

Shown here: Quince & Co. Chickadee (100% American wool; 181 yd [166 m]/1¾ oz [50 g]): caspian, 8 (9, 9, 10, 11, 12) skeins.

NEEDLES

Size U.S. 4 (3.5 mm): 32" (80 cm) circular (cir), 16" (40 cm) cir, set of double-pointed (dpn).

Adjust needle size if necessary to obtain the correct gauge.

NOTIONS

Stitch markers (m), 1 distinctive for beg of rnd, 6 removable (rm); 2 stitch holders; waste yarn; tapestry needle.

GAUGE

26 sts and 38 rnds = 4" (10 cm) in Garter Rib st after blocking.

NOTE

— This pullover is worked from the bottom up. Front and back hems are worked flat, then body is joined in the round and worked seamlessly. Sleeves are worked downward from shoulder stitches using a perpendicular join. I-cord is applied as finishing.

Garter Rib Stitch (back worked flat)

(multiple of 6 sts + 3)

Row 1: (RS) Knit.

Row 2: *P3, k3; rep from * to last 3 sts, p3.

Garter Rib Stitch (front worked flat)

(multiple of 6 sts + 3)

Row 1: (RS) Knit.

Row 2: *K3, p3; rep from * to last 3 sts, k3.

Garter Rib Stitch (worked in the round)

(multiples of 6 sts)

Rnd 1 and all odd-numbered rnds: Knit.

Rnd 2 and all even-numbered rnds: *K3, p3; rep from * to end.

Instructions

HEM

BACK HEM

With longer cir and long-tail method, CO 117 (129, 141, 153, 171, 183) sts. Work flat in Garter Rib Stitch (see Stitch Guide) until piece measures 6" (15 cm) from CO edge, ending with a WS row. Place sts on waste yarn or stitch holder. Break yarn.

FRONT HEM

With longer cir and long-tail method, CO 117 (129, 141, 153, 171, 183) sts. Work flat in Garter Rib Stitch until piece measures 4" (10 cm) from CO edge, ending with a WS row; turn, work Rnd 1 of Garter Rib Stitch in the round (see Stitch Guide) over 117 (129, 141, 153, 171, 183) sts, pm for side, cont working Garter Rib Stitch over 117 (129, 141, 153, 171, 183) sts held for back, pm for beg of rnd —234 (258, 282, 306, 342, 366) sts.

BODY

Cont in patt until piece measures 20 (20, 20, 22, 22, 22)" (51 [51, 51, 56, 56, 56] cm) from CO edge on back.

Divide for armholes: K12 (12, 12, 15, 15, 15), place 24 (24, 24, 30, 30, 30) sts just worked on stitch holder for left underarm, k93 (105, 117, 123, 141, 153) front sts, place next 24 (24, 24, 30, 30, 30) sts on stitch holder for right underarm, place rem 93 (105, 117, 123, 141, 153) sts on waste yarn and hold for back—93 (105, 117, 123, 141, 153) sts rem for front.

UPPER BODY (WORKED FLAT)

FRONT

Work flat in Garter Rib Stitch as established until piece measures 6½ (7, 7½, 8, 8½, 9)" (16.5 [18, 19, 20.5, 21.5, 23] cm) from underarm, ending with a WS row.

Short-row set-up: Prm 5, 11, and 17 sts in from each armhole edge.

Short-row: *Work in patt to 1 st before last rm, remove rm, sl1, move yarn to front, sl1 back to left needle, turn work, move yarn to front, work in patt to 1 st before last rm, remove rm, sl1, move yarn to back, sl1 back to left needle, turn work, move yarn to back; rep from * until all rm have been removed, work in patt until there are 18 (22, 28, 30, 36, 42) sts on right needle, BO 57 (61, 61, 63, 69, 69) center sts, place rem sts on stitch holders for shoulders—18 (22, 28, 30, 36, 42) sts for each shoulder. Break yarn.

BACK

Work as for front.

Join shoulders: Place sts held for shoulders onto dpns. With RS tog and WS facing you, work three-needle bind-off (see Techniques) across one shoulder. Break yarn. Rep for other shoulder.

SLEEVES (MAKE 2)

Using shorter cir, with RS facing and beg at left edge of underarm sts, pick up and knit 87 (93, 99, 111, 117, 123) sts along vertical edge of armhole. Underarm sts remain unworked.

PERPENDICULAR JOIN (WORKED FLAT)

Place underarm sts onto dpns. Turn work so that WS is facing.

Set-up row: (WS) Sl1 wyf, p2, *k3, p3; rep from * to last 6 sts, k3, p2, sl last st to dpn, p2tog, turn—1 underarm st dec'd.

Row 1: (RS) Sl1 wyb, knit to last st, sl last st to dpn, ssk, turn—1 underarm st dec'd.

Row 2: Sl1 wyf, work in patt to last st, sl last st to dpn, p2tog, turn—1 underarm st dec'd.

Rep last 2 rows until 1 underarm st rem.

Next row: Sl1 wyb, knit to 1 st before end, sl1, knit last underarm st tog with first st on left needle, psso. Place rm in this final st, moving it up each rnd, and beg working in the rnd —86 (92, 98, 110, 116, 122) sts.

Work 3 rnds even in patt.

Dec rnd: Knit to 1 st before marked st, cdd—2 sts dec'd.

Rep Dec rnd every 6th rnd 15 (18, 18, 21, 21, 21) more times—54 (54, 60, 66, 72, 78) sts. Work even in patt until sleeve measures 16½ (17, 17, 17½, 17½, 18)" (42 [43, 43, 44.5, 44.5, 45.5] cm) from armpit. Break yarn.

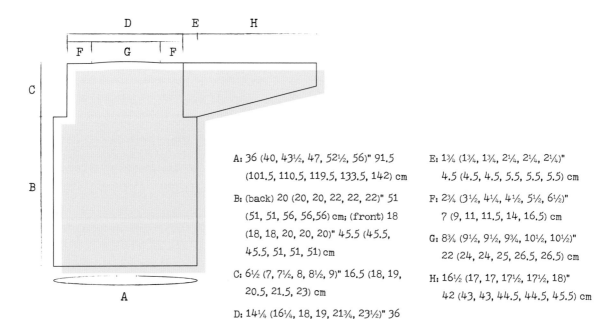

A: 36 (40, 43½, 47, 52½, 56)" 91.5 (101.5, 110.5, 119.5, 133.5, 142) cm

B: (back) 20 (20, 20, 22, 22, 22)" 51 (51, 51, 56, 56,56) cm; (front) 18 (18, 18, 20, 20, 20)" 45.5 (45.5, 45.5, 51, 51, 51) cm

C: 6½ (7, 7½, 8, 8½, 9)" 16.5 (18, 19, 20.5, 21.5, 23) cm

D: 14¼ (16¼, 18, 19, 21¾, 23½)" 36 (41.5, 45.5, 48.5, 55, 59.5) cm

E: 1¾ (1¾, 1¾, 2¼, 2¼, 2¼)" 4.5 (4.5, 4.5, 5.5, 5.5, 5.5) cm

F: 2¾ (3½, 4¼, 4½, 5½, 6½)" 7 (9, 11, 11.5, 14, 16.5) cm

G: 8¾ (9½, 9½, 9¾, 10½, 10½)" 22 (24, 24, 25, 26.5, 26.5) cm

H: 16½ (17, 17, 17½, 17½, 18)" 42 (43, 43, 44.5, 44.5, 45.5) cm

I-CORD BIND-OFF

Using dpn, CO 4 sts; slide sts to other end of dpn, work I-cord bind-off (see Techniques) over rem sleeve sts. BO 4 I-cord sts.

FINISHING

Using dpn, CO 4 sts. With RS facing and beg at top of hem opening on left hip, work applied I-cord (see Techniques) along edge of back hem, working toward lower corner. Work 3 rows applied I-cord into lower corner to turn I-cord edge. Cont working applied I-cord across bottom edge of back, working 3 rows applied I-cord into corner. Cont working applied I-cord to top of hem opening on right hip. BO I-cord sts and break yarn. In this manner, work 4-st applied I-cord along front hem. BO I-cord sts and break yarn. With RS facing and beg at left shoulder join, work 4-st applied I-cord around neck edge. BO I-cord sts and break yarn. Sew together or tack down I-cord ends on collar and sleeve cuffs so that the joins are as invisible as possible. Weave in ends. Wet-block piece to finished measurements.

KINDRED SPIRITS: WHEN KNITTERS FIND KNITTERS, MAGIC HAPPENS

by Shannon Cook

IN LIFE, WE ALL STRIVE to learn our true identity. We also find out what our passions are, which hobbies and activities we love, and which are the ones that we just can't imagine living without. One of the best parts of finding a passion is getting to share your joy with others, and—even better—with a good friend.

For those whose passion is knitting, the simple act of working with two sticks and some string has the power not just to make something, but also to evoke emotion, tell a story, and forge relationships. The story that knitting tells starts with the fiber—where and how it was made. The story develops as the knitter makes the piece and then finally gives it to the recipient. And when knitters get to know each other, something magical happens, and these stories of making and gifting start to intertwine.

There's nothing else quite like making a knitter friend. That moment when someone just "gets you" and knows why you love the smell of wool, why you stay up all night to knit until your hands give out. Knitting starts conversations that bridge age, ethnicity, and gender.

If you're knitting and find yourself lonely, look no further. There is always a wealth of amazingly loving and kind people just waiting to be found. The knitting community can be warm and comforting, akin to a giant hug. I'm constantly amazed at the strength, resilience, and talents of this community of makers. Knitters are giving, loving, and generous folk. They protect each other like your favorite woolly blanket blocks the chill from your bones.

I mean, who else can you squeal with delight with over your newest needles or that fabulous new yarn dyer you found? Who else will want to see endless pictures of your knitting (and vice versa), chat pattern choices for hours, and hunt down that elusive perfect knitting bag with you? A knitter friend will. They'll cheer you on through every row, hold you up when you have to frog, help you pick which color works best for you, and be so proud when that finished project exceeds both your expectations! It's a special kind of friendship, and one that every knitter should have.

Put yourself out there! I know it can be scary, but so is life, and you don't want to miss out on that. Join a Ravelry group or a knit along, start chatting on Instagram, visit your local yarn shop and take a class or participate in a knit night; heck, sometimes it's as simple as pulling out your knitting in a waiting room or on a bus to find a fellow knitter. Because making a knitting friend is a gift, it's good for the soul. A perfect latte will perk you up, and your new friend will awaken your inner smile and energize you in a way that you couldn't possibly imagine. Knitting is enjoyable solo, but it can also be way more fun with a friend.

So, just like that new skein of yarn is waiting to be held and turned into something beautiful, there is another knitter just waiting to be found, a cup of coffee just waiting to be shared, along with stitches to be knit and friendships to be made.

Just look for the magic in the sticks and the string. —

When knitters get to know each other, something magical happens, and these stories of making and gifting start to intertwine.

KAFFEE

This fun, quick unisex hat is full of texture and relaxing to knit. Twisted rib and an allover stitch pattern make this stylish hat a great choice to make while having conversations, bingeing TV, and more! You can experiment with colors, fibers, and pom-pom size (if you want one at all—try making one without and see if you like it!) I promise you will want more than just one. So go ahead, cast one on and enjoy that cup of coffee with a friend. — **SHANNON COOK**

FINISHED SIZE

About 16 (17, 18)" (40.5 [43, 45.5] cm) unstretched brim circumference, and 9½ (10, 10½)" (24 [25.5, 26.5] cm) high.

Project shown measures 16" (40.5 cm).

YARN

DK weight (#3 light).

Shown here: Brooklyn Tweed Arbor (100% Targhee wool; 145 yd [133 m]/1¾ oz [50 g]): parka, 2 skeins.

NEEDLES

Size U.S. 5 (3.75 mm): 16" (40 cm) circular (cir) for brim.

Size U.S. 6 (4 mm): 16" (40 cm) cir for hat body; set of double-pointed (dpn), 32" (80 cm) cir for magic loop method, or 2 cir for crown.

Adjust needle size if necessary to obtain the correct gauge.

NOTIONS

Stitch marker (m); tapestry needle; pom-pom maker (optional).

GAUGE

20 sts and 28 rnds = 4" (10 cm) in Reverse Stockinette st with larger needle, unblocked.

22 sts and 32 rnds = 4" (10 cm) in Twisted Rib with smaller needle, unblocked.

K1L: Bring working yarn to back of work, insert needle into stitch 2 rows below next stitch and knit 1, drop unworked stitch above.

1x1 ribbed long-tail cast-on: Make a slipknot and place it on the right-hand needle, leaving a long tail. Place the thumb and index finger of your left hand between the two threads. Secure the long ends with your other three fingers. Hold your hand palm up and spread your thumb and index finger apart to make a V of the yarn around them. You have four strands of yarn: 1, 2, 3, and 4 **(Figure 1)**. Place the needle under strand 1, from front to back.

Place the needle over the top of strand 3 **(Figure 2)** and bring the needle down through the loop around your thumb **(Figure 3)**. Drop the loop off your thumb and, placing your thumb back in the V configuration, tighten up the resulting stitch on the needle.

Place the needle under strand 4, from back to front.

Place the needle over the top of strand 2 **(Figure 4)** and bring the needle back through the loop around your index finger.

Drop the loop off your index finger **(Figure 5)** and, placing your index finger back in the V configuration, tighten up the resulting stitch on the needle.

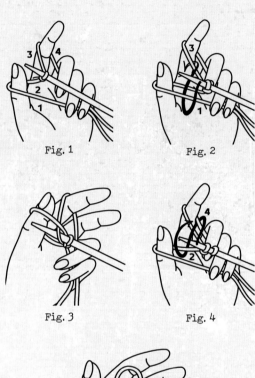

Fig. 1

Fig. 2

Fig. 3

Fig. 4

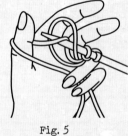

Fig. 5

Instructions

BRIM

With smaller needle, CO 112 (116, 120) sts using the 1x1 ribbed long-tail cast-on (see Stitch Guide). Pm and join for working in the round, being careful not to twist.

Rnd 1: *K1 tbl, p1; rep from * to end.

Rep Rnd 1 until work measures 2" (5 cm) from CO edge, or desired length.

BODY

Switch to larger needle.

SET-UP RND
Size 16" (40.5 cm) only

Next rnd: *P2, p2tog; rep from * to end—84 sts.

Size 17" (43 cm) only

Next rnd: *P2, p2tog; rep from * to last 4 sts, p4—88 sts.

Size 18" (45.5 cm) only

Next rnd: *[P2, p2tog] 7 times, p2; rep from * to end—92 sts.

All Sizes

Rnds 1, 2, 4, 5, and 6: Purl.

Rnd 3: *K1L, p3; rep from * to end.

Rnd 7: P2, *k1L, p3; rep from * to last 2 sts, k1L, p1.

Rnd 8: Purl.

Sizes 16 (18)" (40.5 [45.5] cm) only

Work Rnds 1–8 of of Body 4 (5) more times.

Continue to Crown Shaping.

Size 17" (43 cm) only

Work Rnds 1–8 of Body 4 more times.

Work Rnds 1–4 once.

Continue to Crown Shaping.

CROWN SHAPING

If using a 16" (40 cm) circular needle, switch to dpn or preferred small-circumference needle when work becomes too small to comfortably fit on your circular needle.

Size 16" (40.5 cm) only

Rnd 1: *P10, k2tog; rep from * to end—77 sts.

Rnd 2: *P10, k1; rep from * to end.

Rnd 3: *[K1L, p3] twice, k1L, k2tog; rep from * to end—70 sts.

Rnd 4: *P9, k1, rep from * to end.

Rnd 5: *P8, k2tog; rep from * to end—63 sts.

Rnd 6: *P8, k1; rep from * to end.

Rnd 7: *P2, k1L, p3, k1L, k2tog; rep from * to end—56 sts.

Rnd 8: *P7, k1; rep from * to end.

Rnd 9: *P6, k2tog; rep from * to end—49 sts.

Rnd 10: *P6, k1; rep from * to end.

Rnd 11: *K1L, p3, k1L, k2tog; rep from * to end—42 sts.

Rnd 12: *P5, k1; rep from * to end.

Rnd 13: *P4, k2tog; rep from * to end—35 sts.

Rnd 14: *P3, k2tog; rep from * to end—28 sts.

Rnd 15: *P1, k1L, k2tog; rep from * to end—21 sts.

Rnd 16: *P1, k2tog; rep from * to end—14 sts.

Size 17" (43 cm) only

Rnd 1: *P9, k2tog; rep from * to end—80 sts.

Rnd 2: *P9, k1; rep from * to end.

Rnd 3: *P2, k1L, p3, k1L, p1, k2tog; rep from * to end—72 sts.

Rnd 4: *P8, k1; rep from * to end.

Rnd 5: *P7, k2tog; rep from * to end—64 sts.

Rnd 6: *P7, k1; rep from * to end.

Rnd 7: *K1L, p3, k1L, p1, k2tog; rep from * to end—56 sts.

Rnd 8: *P6, k1; rep from * to end.

Rnd 9: *P5, k2tog; rep from * to end—48 sts.

Rnd 10: *P5, k1; rep from * to end.

Rnd 11: *P2, k1L, p1, k2tog; rep from * to end—40 sts.

Rnd 12: *P4, k1; rep from * to end.

Rnd 13: *P3, k2tog; rep from * to end—32 sts.

Rnd 14: *P2, k2tog; rep from * to end—24 sts.

Rnd 15: *K1L, k2tog; rep from * to end—16 sts.

Rnd 16: *K2tog; rep from * to end—8 sts.

Size 18" (45.5 cm) only

Rnd 1: K2tog, purl to last 2 sts, k2tog—90 sts.

Rnd 2: Purl to end.

Rnd 3: *[P3, k1L] twice, k2tog; rep from * to end—81 sts.

Rnd 4: *P8, k1; rep from * to end.

Rnd 5: *P7, k2tog; rep from * to end—72 sts.

Rnd 6: *P7, k1; rep from * to end.

Rnd 7: *P1, k1L, p3, k1L, k2tog; rep from * to end—63 sts.

Rnd 8: *P6, k1; rep from * to end.

Rnd 9: *P5, k2tog; rep from * to end—54 sts.

Rnd 10: *P5, k1; rep from * to end.

Rnd 11: *P3, k1L, k2tog; rep from * to end—45 sts.

Rnd 12: *P4, k1; rep from * to end.

Rnd 13: *P3, k2tog; rep from * to end—36 sts.

Rnd 14: *P3, k1; rep from * to end.

Rnd 15: *P1, k1L, k2tog; rep from * to end—27 sts.

Rnd 16: *P1, k2tog; rep from * to end—18 sts.

Rnd 17: *K2tog; rep from * to end—9 sts.

FINISHING

Hat should now measure about 9½ (10, 10½)" (25 [26.5, 28] cm) from CO edge.

Cut yarn, leaving a 6" (15 cm) tail. Use tapestry needle to thread tail through remaining sts and pull tight to close. Weave in ends (or leave tail loose if attaching a matching pom-pom; see Techniques for making a pom-pom) and wet-block your hat to finished measurements.

FLAT WHITE *Cowl*

Get your colorwork fix with this quick and striking cowl. Bold neutrals in a heavy worsted yarn make this a go-with-everything accessory for the winter months. It's a great first colorwork project, too! The purl ridges between ribbing and colorwork sections can act as a turning row for an alternate way of styling the cowl. Just turn one or both ribbing sections to the inside of the cowl for a shorter cowl or to emphasize the colorwork. — **ANDREA RANGEL**

FINISHED SIZE
About 18" (45.5 cm) circumference, and 9¼" (23.5 cm) high.

YARN
Worsted weight (#4 medium).

Shown here: YOTH Father (100% Rambouillet wool; 220 yd [201 m]/3½ oz [100 g]): cider (MC), 1 skein; hazelnut (CC), 1 skein.

NEEDLES
Size U.S. 7 (4.5 mm).

Adjust needle size if necessary to obtain the correct gauge.

NOTIONS
Stitch marker (m); tapestry needle.

GAUGE
20 sts and 24 rnds = 4" (10 cm) in Radius patt after blocking.

NOTES
— Cowl is worked in the round from bottom to top.

— If you find your colorwork section is drawing in compared to the ribbing, use a larger needle size over two-color rounds.

— Hold the Contrast Color dominant throughout the two-color section of this cowl.

— There's no need to catch floats during this color chart, but to improve even tension and avoid bunching, spread the stitches out on the right needle (the stitches already worked) as you work.

Instructions

RIBBED EDGE

With MC and using long-tail cast-on method, CO 88 sts. Pm and join for working in the round, being careful not to twist.

Rnd 1: *K2, p2; rep from * to end.

Rep Rnd 1 eleven more times, until ribbing measures about 2" (5 cm) from CO.

Purl 1 rnd.

Next rnd: (inc) M1, k44, M1, knit to end—90 sts.

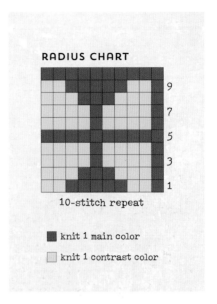

RADIUS CHART

9

7

5

3

1

10-stitch repeat

■ knit 1 main color

□ knit 1 contrast color

COLORWORK CENTER

Join CC1. Work from chart using MC and CC as follows:

Rnd 1: [Work 10-st Radius Chart] 9 times across the rnd.

Last round establishes the colorwork pattern. Continue working from Radius Chart as established, working Rnds 1–10 twice, then Rnds 1–9 once more.

RIBBED EDGE

Next rnd: (dec) K44, k2tog, k38, k2tog, knit to end—88 sts.

Purl 1 rnd.

Next rnd: *K2, p2; rep from * to end.

Rep last rnd eleven more times, until ribbing measures about 2" (5 cm) from purl ridge.

BO all stitches in pattern.

FINISHING

Weave in ends using duplicate stitch on the WS and wet-block.

Marshmallow TEE

This tee is the perfect project for knitting over coffee because it doesn't require any shaping, counting, or complex pattern stitches. Its simplicity allows the yarn to bring interest and life to your garment. The silky, shiny thin fiber contrasts with the soft matte poof of the thick fiber (which reminds me so much of marshmallows!), and this yarn's texture has the added benefit of hiding any uneven knitting tension. — **AMY ROLLIS**

FINISHED SIZE

About 20" (51 cm) across the back and 17" (43 cm) high.

YARN

Thick-and-thin bulky weight (#5 bulky).

Shown here: Universal Yarn Bamboo Bloom (48% bamboo, 44% wool, 8% acrylic; 154 yd [141 m]/3½ oz [100 g]): 206 jasmine, 3 balls.

NEEDLES

Size U.S. 10½ (6.5 mm).

Adjust needle size if necessary to obtain the correct gauge.

NOTIONS

Tapestry needle.

GAUGE

13 sts and 26 rows = 4" (10 cm) in garter st after blocking.

NOTES

— If other thick-and-thin yarn is substituted work in one needle size larger than its label recommends.

— Working in the larger size is easier on your hands and produces a fabric with more drape for the half twist.

— Given the uneven yarn texture and oversized fit, exact gauge is not critical, but size can be adjusted by casting on more or fewer stitches. Just remember to cast on the same number of stitches for both the front and back pieces.

— Slipping the first stitch of every row purlwise creates a neater fabric edge.

— For easier seaming, use a non-slubby yarn of the same color and similar fiber content.

— The pattern is written to accommodate a variety of sizes by its loose fit. The tee is worked entirely in easy, reversible garter stitch. Front and back are knit sideways, separately. For a slimming feature, the front is knit slightly longer to allow for a one-half twist of the fabric before simple seaming forms the neck and cap sleeves, keeping the tee in place on your shoulders. You'll quickly have a stylish and modern go-anywhere wardrobe piece, or a thoughtful gift for a friend.

Instructions

BACK

Loosely CO 56 sts.

Row 1: Sl1, knit to end.

Rep this row until piece measures 20" (51 cm) from cast-on edge.

BO loosely.

FRONT

Loosely CO 56 sts.

Row 1: Sl1, knit to end.

Rep this row until piece measures 28" (71 cm) from cast-on edge.

BO loosely.

FINISHING

Lightly dampen and gently block pieces.

SEAM SIDES

The 17" (43 cm) cast-on and bind-off edges of both pieces will form the sides of the garment. The longer piece is the front. Lay front on top of back, aligning the right side edges. From bottom right corner, measure up 3" (7.5 cm) (hip vent) and start seaming the sides for 5" (12.5 cm). Where you stop will be the underarm opening. Hold the left edge of the longer front piece, make a one-half twist, and line up the left edges of both pieces in the same way you did for the first side. From bottom left corner, measure 3" (7.5 cm) for hip vent and seam 5" (12.5 cm) of the edges together as before.

SEAM SHOULDERS

From top left outside corner, seam toward neck for 6" (15 cm). Seam right shoulder in the same way.

Weave in ends and enjoy!

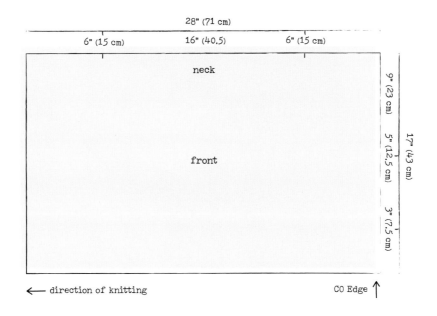

28" (71 cm)

6" (15 cm)   16" (40,5)   6" (15 cm)

neck

front

9" (23 cm)

5" (12.5 cm)

3" (7.5 cm)

17" (43 cm)

← direction of knitting   CO Edge ↑

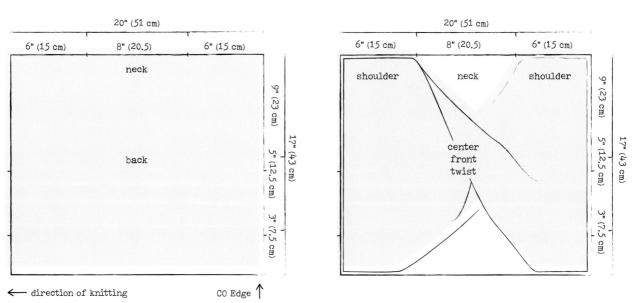

20" (51 cm)

6" (15 cm)   8" (20,5)   6" (15 cm)

neck

back

9" (23 cm)

5" (12.5 cm)

3" (7.5 cm)

17" (43 cm)

← direction of knitting   CO Edge ↑

20" (51 cm)

6" (15 cm)   8" (20,5)   6" (15 cm)

shoulder   neck   shoulder

center
front
twist

9" (23 cm)

5" (12.5 cm)

3" (7.5 cm)

17" (43 cm)

Dirty Chai PULLOVER

Sugar and spice and everything nice, that's what dirty chai lattes (and essential knits) are made of. The swirling, traveling-stitch yoke of the Dirty Chai Pullover mimics steam rising from your favorite hot drink, with enough drape and ease for a comforting and flattering fit. The top-down construction, split hem, and near-tunic-length silhouette make for a relaxing afternoon in a coffee shop on a chilly day. — **MEGHAN BABIN**

ıı ı ı ıı ıı ı ıı ı ıı ı ıı ıı ıı ı ıı ı ıı ı ıı ı ı ı ıı ıı ı

FINISHED SIZE

About 39 (43, 47, 51¼, 55½, 59¾, 63¼)" (99 [109, 119.5, 130, 141, 152, 160.5) cm] bust circumference.

Designed to have about 6–10" (15–25.5 cm) of positive ease.

Garment shown measures 43" (109 cm), modeled with 9" (23 cm) of ease.

YARN

Worsted weight (#4 medium).

Shown here: Woolfolk FÅR (100% Ovis 21 Ultimate Merino wool; 143 yd [130 m]/1¾ oz [50 g]): #18, 8 (10, 12, 14, 16, 18, 20) skeins.

NEEDLES

Size U.S. 8 (5 mm): 32" (80 cm) circular (cir), 16" (40 cm) cir, set of double-pointed (dpn).

Size U.S. 7 (4.5 mm): 32" (80 cm) cir, set of dpn.

Adjust needle size if necessary to obtain the correct gauge.

NOTIONS

Stitch markers (m), 1 distinctive for beg of rnd; cable needle (cn); waste yarn; tapestry needle.

GAUGE

19 sts and 28 rnds = 4" (10 cm) in Stockinette st on larger needle after blocking.

NOTE

— Back and front hems are worked flat on long circular needle.

STITCH GUIDE

1/1 Left Twist (1/1LT):
Insert right needle
into second st on left
needle tbl and knit
without removing
from needle, then
insert right needle
into first stitch on left
needle and knit; drop
both sts just worked
from left needle.

**1/1 Left Cable
Increase (1/1LC
inc):** Slip 1 st to cable
needle and hold
to front, k1f&b, k1
from cable needle
—1 st inc'd.

Instructions

YOKE

With larger 16" (40 cm) cir needle, CO 96 sts (for all sizes). Pm and join for working in the round, being careful not to twist.

Set-up rnd: *K4, pm; rep from * to end.

||||||||||||||||||||||||||||||||||||||||||||||||

NOTE: *Throughout yoke, the beginning of the round shifts one stitch to the left every cable round.*

||||||||||||||||||||||||||||||||||||||||||||||||

Sizes 39" and 43" (99 and 109 cm) only

**Rnd 1: *Knit to 1 st before m, sl1, remove m, sl st back to left needle, 1/1LT (see Stitch Guide), replace m; rep from * to end.

Rnd 2: Knit to end.

Rep Rnds 1 and 2 two more times.

Inc rnd A: *Knit to 1 st before m, sl1, remove m, sl st back to left needle, 1/1LC inc (see Stitch Guide), replace m; rep from * to end—24 sts inc'd.

Rnd 3: Knit to end.

Rnd 4: *Knit to 1 st before m, sl1, remove m, sl st back to left needle, 1/1LT, replace m; rep from * to end.

Rep Rnds 3 and 4 two more times.

Inc rnd B: *Knit to 1 st before m, k1f&b; rep from * to end—24 sts inc'd.**

Rep from ** to ** 3 (4, -, -, -, -, -, -) more times—288 (336, -, -, -, -, -, -) sts.

Size 39" (99 cm) only

Rep Rnds 1 and 2 three more times.

Inc rnd A: *Knit to 1 st before m, sl1, remove m, sl st back to left needle, 1/1LC inc, replace m; rep from * to end—312 sts.

Size 47" (119.5 cm) only

**Rnd 1: *Knit to 1 st before m, sl1, remove m, sl st back to left needle, 1/1LT (see Stitch Guide), replace m; rep from * to end.

Rnd 2: Knit to end.

Rep Rnds 1 and 2 once more.

Inc rnd A: *Knit to 1 st before m, sl1, remove m, sl st back to left needle, 1/1LC inc (see Stitch Guide), replace m; rep from * to end—24 sts inc'd.

Next rnd: Knit to end.**

Rep from ** to ** 6 more times—264 sts.

***Rep Rnds 1 and 2 three times.

Inc rnd A: *Knit to 1 st before m, sl1, remove m, sl st back to left needle, 1/1LC inc, replace m; rep from * to end—24 sts inc'd.

Rnd 3: Knit to end.

Rnd 4: *Knit to 1 st before m, sl1, remove m, sl st back to left needle, 1/1LT, replace m; rep from * to end.

Rep Rnds 3 and 4 two more times.

Inc rnd B: *Knit to 1 st before m, k1f&b; rep from * to end—24 sts inc'd.***

Rep from *** to *** once more—360 sts.

Sizes 51¼", 55½", and 59¾" (130, 141, and 152 cm) only

**Rnd 1: *Knit to 1 st before m, sl1, remove m, sl st back to left needle, 1/1LT (see Stitch Guide), replace m; rep from * to end.

Rnd 2: Knit to end.

Rep Rnds 1 and 2 once more.

Inc rnd A: *Knit to 1 st before m, sl1, remove m, sl st back to left needle, 1/1LC inc (see Stitch Guide), replace m; rep from * to end—24 sts inc'd.

Next rnd: Knit to end.**

Rep from ** to ** - (-, -, 11, 12, 13, -) more times—- (-, -, 384, 408, 432, -) sts.

Size 63¼" (160.5 cm) only

**Rnd 1: *Knit to 1 st before m, sl1, remove m, sl st back to left needle, 1/1LT (see Stitch Guide), replace m; rep from * to end.

Rnd 2: Knit to end.

Rep Rnds 1 and 2 once more.

Inc rnd A: *Knit to 1 st before m, sl1, remove m, sl st back to left needle, 1/1LC inc (see Stitch Guide), replace m; rep from * to end—24 sts inc'd.

Rnd 3: Knit to end.

Rnd 4: *Knit to 1 st before m, sl1, remove m, sl st back to left needle, 1/1LT, replace m; rep from * to end.

Rep Rnds 3 and 4 once more.

Inc rnd B: *Knit to 1 st before m, k1f&b; rep from * to end —24 sts inc'd.**

Rep from ** to ** 2 more times—240 sts.

***Rep Rnds 1 and 2 two times.

Inc rnd A: *Knit to 1 st before m, sl1, remove m, sl st back to left needle, 1/1LC inc, replace m; rep from * to end—24 sts inc'd.

Next rnd: Knit to end.***

Rep from *** to *** 8 more times—456 sts.

All sizes

Work even in St st until yoke measures 9 (10, 10½, 11, 11½, 12, 12½)" (23 [25.5, 26.5, 28, 29, 30.5, 31.5] cm) from CO edge.

DIVIDE FOR BODY AND SLEEVES

*Transfer 64 (66, 68, 70, 72, 74, 78) sts to waste yarn, rejoin for working in the round and k92 (102, 112, 122, 132, 142, 150); rep from * to end—184 (204, 224, 244, 264, 284, 300) sts; 64 (66, 68, 70, 72, 74, 78) sts held for each sleeve.

BODY

Work in St st until body measures 12 (12½, 13, 13½, 14, 14½, 15)" (30.5 [31.5, 33, 34.5, 35.5, 37, 38] cm) from underarm.

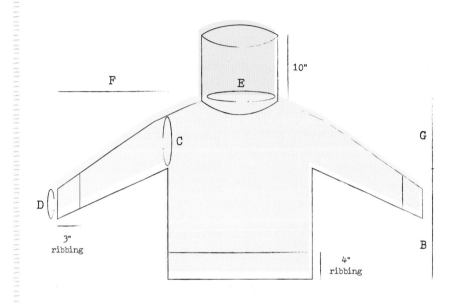

A: 38¾ (43, 47¼, 51¼, 55½, 59¾, 63¼)" 98.5 (109, 122.5, 130, 152, 160.5) cm

B: 12 (12½, 13, 13½, 14, 14½, 15)" 30.5 (31.5, 33, 34.5, 35.5, 38) cm

C: 13½ (14, 14¼, 14¾, 15¼, 15½, 16½)" 34.5 (35.5, 36, 37.5, 38.5, 39.5, 42) cm

D: 8½ (8¾, 9¼, 9¾, 10, 10½, 10½)" 21.5 (22, 23.5, 25, 25.5, 26.5, 26.5) cm

E: 20¼" 51.5 cm

F: 15½ (16, 16, 16, 16½, 16½, 16½)" 39.5 (40.5, 40.5, 40.5, 42, 42, 42) cm

G: 9 (10, 10½, 11, 11½, 12, 12½)" 23 (25.5, 26.5, 28, 29, 30.5, 31.5) cm

Divide for front and back hems:
K2tog, k90 (100, 110, 120, 130, 140, 148), place sts just worked on waste yarn; k2tog, knit to end—2 sts dec'd, 91 (101, 111, 121, 131, 141, 149) sts rem for back and front.

FRONT HEM
Change to smaller 32" (80 cm) cir needle and work in 1x1 rib as follows:

Row 1: (WS) Sl1, *k1, p1; rep from * to end.

Row 2: (RS) Sl1, *p1, k1; rep from * to end.

Rep Rows 1 and 2 until ribbing measures 4" (10 cm), ending after Row 1. BO all sts.

BACK HEM
Transfer held back sts onto smaller 32" (80 cm) cir needle. Join yarn ready to work a WS row, and work as for front hem.

SLEEVES (MAKE 2)
Transfer held sleeve sts onto larger 16" (40 cm) cir needle, pm and join for working in the round. Change to dpn when circumference becomes too small to work on 16" (40 cm) cir.

**Work in St st for 6 (6, 6, 6, 6, 6, 5) rnds.

Dec rnd: K1, k2tog, work in St st to last 3 sts, ssk, k1—2 sts dec'd.

Rep from ** 11 (11, 11, 11, 11, 13) more times. Work in St st until sleeve measures 12½ (13, 13, 13, 13½, 13½, 13½)" (31.5 [33, 33, 33, 34.5, 34.5, 34.5] cm) from underarm—40 (42, 44, 46, 48, 50, 50) sts remain.

Change to smaller needle and work in 1x1 rib as follows:

Rnd 1: *K1, p1; rep from * to end.

Rep Rnd 1 until ribbing measures 3" (7.5 cm). BO all sts.

COWL NECK

With larger 16" (40 cm) cir needle, beg at center back neck, pick up and knit 96 sts, matching pick-ups to neckline sts as closely as possible. Pm and join for working in the round.

Rnd 1: *K1, p1; rep from * to end.

Rep Rnd 1 until cowl neck measures 10" (25.5 cm) or desired length. BO all sts.

FINISHING

Seam underarm gaps. Weave in ends. Wet-block pullover to finished measurements.

THE RITUAL OF KNIT NIGHT

by Hannah Thiessen

NOT EVERY KNIT NIGHT begins with a ritual, although perhaps the best ones do. The beginning signal might be the click of an electric kettle or the bubbling noise of a coffee pot's industrious percolation. Maybe the ritual of knit night begins with a door chime, an announcement that the first of the knitters has arrived, laden with project bag or basket. A weary traveler settles into the arms of a welcoming chair. Soon other members arrive in a flurry of coats, shawls, and scarves, settling into this special space made ready for them. The warm glow of the shop highlights friendly faces, familiar and fresh, that have come united around a single purpose: to feel rejuvenated and loved.

This night begins with a round of show and tell. Projects are pulled from the depths of our bags, and we celebrate the changes in every project. Progress is progress, no matter how small, and every inch of simple Stockinette or row of beaded lace is fondled and respected. Newly started pieces are fussed over, and the yarn information is shared; skeins are passed about and pointed out on nearby store shelves. Those casting on will discover ample help among the collective mind of the group, eager to recommend the best method or discuss the nuances of different choices. Equal opportunity is given to projects that have not yet begun: a question for feedback on color, fit, or yarn choice is put to a vote. The group is a mirror for us, a community of individuals on which we may rely and trust to help us make only the best decisions. There are no strangers here, only friends we have not yet encountered. Late arrivals are greeted and bags shuffled to make space for new chairs and projects.

It's not all about the knitting, though. Often, when the clicking of needles begins, so does the discussion. We use these times to check in, gather the latest news about family members, house renovations, upcoming events, and local gossip. These times are about celebrating small victories and providing encouragement and support for those in deepest need of it. Should the discussion turn polarizing or political, knitters find themselves more open to share and discuss civilly, our shoulders and minds already relaxed in the repeating meditation of every stitch. We know that while these issues are important to us, the community of our knit night is also a delicate, beautiful thing; and we seek to maintain the balance of a comfortable space to which we can escape from all the complications of the outside world. Prejudice, hatred, and dissention are unwelcome, in favor of connection, understanding, and mutual respect.

Time seems to slow in these sacred hours, progressing in the steady form of rows gained. Conversation rises and slows, but never stalls; momentary silence is a space for counting, checking in, reviewing patterns. A finished project is exalted by all, the owner made to stand up and model it under the approving gaze of the group. This is a truly safe space—a place where we can be together for a few hours without the binding obligations of the everyday—and when it comes to a close, there is an unspoken understanding that it is not lost, simply put on hold until the next opportunity arises.

When at last the time comes, the final signal of the evening is a gathering of notions and needles, the folding of a project back into a bag. The group's collective well-wishes rise and fade as each member departs. As people leave, they take a little of the warm glow of the evening home with them, a reminder that even when the world outside is unyielding, dark, and unknown, there is always the bright spot that is knit night. —

This is a truly safe space—a place where we can be together for a few hours without the binding obligations of the everyday.

TASSEOGRAPHY *Cowl*

Since medieval times, fortune-tellers have been looking to the bottom of teacups to gaze into the future. As I worked this simple six-stitch-repeat cowl, the smattering of the hand-dyed speckles reminded me of reading tea leaves. While I'm not an expert in tasseography (reading tea leaves), I suspect you'll love the simplicity of the stitches, the beautiful drape and hand of the fabric, and the wearability of this finished design. I see knitting in your future. — **KERRY BOGERT**

FINISHED SIZE
About 9" (23 cm) wide and 68½" (174 cm) around.

YARN
Worsted weight (#4 medium).

Shown here: Western Sky Knits Magnolia Worsted (80% superwash Merino wool, 10% cashmere, 10% nylon; 200 yd [183 m]/4 oz [115 g]): birch bark, 3 skeins.

NEEDLES
Size U.S. 9 (5.5 mm): 40" (100 cm) circular (cir).

Adjust needle size if necessary to obtain the correct gauge.

NOTIONS
Tapestry needle.

GAUGE
14 sts and 27 rnds = 4" (10 cm) in patt after blocking.

NOTES
— By using a total stitch count of a multiple of six plus one, the six-stitch repeat is offset by one stitch when working in the round. This offset creates a natural spiral effect that does not require a beginning or end of the round.

Instructions

Using the long-tail method, CO 241 sts. Join for working in the round, being careful not to twist.

*K3, yo, p2tog, p1. Rep from * until cowl measures about 9" (23 cm) from CO edge.

ALT INSTRUCTIONS FOR WORKING IN RNDS OR CHARTED

Using the long-tail cast-on, CO 241 sts. Pm and join for knitting in the round, being careful not to twist.

NOTE: *Sl m at the end of each rnd, except for Rnd 4.*

Rnd 1: *K3, yo, p2tog, p1; rep from * until 1 st remains, k1.

Rnd 2: K2, yo, p2tog, p1, *k3, yo, p2tog, p1; rep from * until 2 sts remain, k2.

Rnd 3: K1, yo, p2tog, p1, *k3, yo, p2tog, p1; rep from * until 3 sts remain, k3.

Rnd 4: Yo, p2tog, p1, *k3, yo, p2tog, p1; rep from * until 4 sts remain, k3, sl1, remove m, return slipped st to left needle, yo, p2tog, replace m.

Rnd 5: P1, *k3, yo, p2tog, p1; rep from * to end.

Repeat Rnds 1–5 eleven more times, or until cowl measures about 9" (23 cm) from CO edge.

FINISHING

BO loosely in patt, working yo's as purl sts.

Block to finished measurements.

Weave in ends.

TASSEOGRAPHY CHART

		knit			p2tog
		purl			no stitch
		yo			repeat

CHOCOLATE CHALLAH *Pullover*

This comfortable sweater exudes effortlessness, thanks to the wonderful drape and hand of the Suri alpaca and wool blend. This piece has an unusual construction: the body is knit in one piece up to the underarm, then split into an apex-V front and solid back; separately knit shoulder panels feature alternating braided cables; and the sleeves are picked up and knit in the round to an elegant bracelet length. — **HANNAH THIESSEN**

FINISHED SIZE

About 32 (34, 36, 38, 40¾, 44, 46) " (81.5 [86.5, 91.5, 96.5, 103.5, 112, 117] cm) bust circumference.

Designed to have about 2–4" (5–10 cm) of positive ease; I recommend 2" (5 cm) ease for smaller sizes and closer to 4" (10 cm) ease for larger sizes, to maintain the oversized shape while allowing for a fuller bust.

Garment shown measures 40¾" (103.5 cm), modeled with 6" (17 cm) of ease.

YARN

Fingering weight (#1 superfine).

Shown here: Salt River Mills Simply Suri (85% alpaca, 15% Merino wool; 330 yd [302 m]/3½ oz [100 g]): chestnut, 4 (4, 5, 5, 5, 6, 6) skeins.

NEEDLES

Size U.S. 3 (3.25 mm): 40" (100 cm) circular (cir) for body and sleeves, 24" (60 cm) cir for neckline.

Adjust needle size if necessary to obtain the correct gauge.

NOTIONS

Stitch markers (m), 2 removable (rm); tapestry needle.

GAUGE

24 sts and 32 rnds = 4" (10 cm) in Stockinette st after blocking.

27 sts and 32 rows = 4" (10 cm) in Alternating Braided Cable after blocking.

NOTES

— It is important to wet-block the cable panels and body to exact measurements for best results; steam-blocking will not achieve as accurate results. I cabled without a cable needle to make the cable panels go quickly, which is a useful technique if you should like to attempt it.

2x2 ribbing in the round

All rounds: *K2, p2; rep from * to end.

Alternating Braided Cable

Row 1: (RS) *P4, k2, 2/2LC, k2, p4, k2, 2/2RC, k2; rep from * to last 16 sts, p4, k2, 2/2LC, k2, p4.

Row 2 and all WS rows: Knit the knit sts and purl the purl sts.

Row 3: *P4, k4, 2/2LC, p4, 2/2RC, k4; rep from * to last 16 sts, p4, k4, 2/2LC, p4.

Row 5: *P4, k2, 2/2RC, k2, p4, k2, 2/2LC, k2; rep from * to last 16 sts, p4, k2, 2/2RC, k2, p4.

Row 7: *P4, 2/2RC, k4, p4, k4, 2/2LC; rep from * to last 16 sts, p4, 2/2RC, k4, p4.

Row 8: Knit the knit sts and purl the purl sts.

2/2LC: Slip 2 stitches onto a cable needle and hold in front, k2, then k2 from the cable needle.

2/2RC: Slip 2 stitches onto a cable needle and hold in back, k2, then k2 from the cable needle.

Instructions

BODY

Using longer cir, CO 192 (204, 216, 228, 244, 264, 276) sts. Pm and join for working in the round, being careful not to twist.

Work in 2x2 ribbing for 1½" (3.8 cm).

Knit in St st for about 14½ (14½, 14½, 16, 16, 16½, 16½)" (37 [37, 37, 40.5, 40.5, 42, 42] cm) or about 116 (116, 116, 128, 128, 132, 132) rnds, then divide for front/back as follows:

K84 (90, 96, 102, 110, 120, 126) back sts, pm, k42 (45, 48, 51, 55, 60, 63), pm for center front short-rows, k24, pm for center front short-rows, k42 (45, 48, 51, 55, 60, 63). The beg of rnd m will be your other side m.

Next rnd: Knit to m, sm, knit to first center front short-row m.

CENTER FRONT SHORT-ROWS

Short-row 1: (RS) K24, turn work.

Short-row 2: (WS) Bring yarn to back, sl1 wyb, bring yarn to front, p23, turn work.

Short-row 3: Bring yarn to front, sl1 wyf, bring yarn to back, knit to the previously wrapped st, turn work.

Short-row 4: Bring yarn to back, sl1 wyb, bring yarn to the front, purl to the previously wrapped st, turn work.

Repeat Short-rows 3 and 4 until you have 12 wrapped sts on each side. The last wrapped st will just be wrapped, with no purling afterward.

Knit to m, picking up and knitting tbl each short-row wrap with the stitch

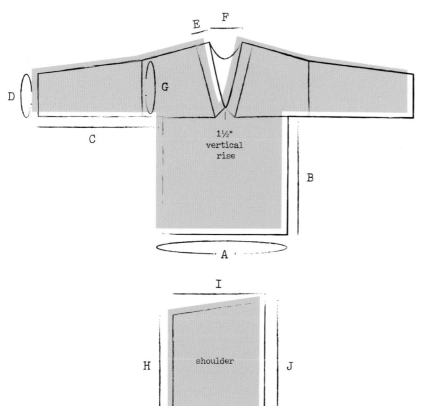

A: 32 (34, 36, 38, 41¾, 44, 46)"
81.5 (86.5, 91.5, 106, 117) cm

B: 14½ (14½, 14½, 16, 16, 16½, 16½)"
37 (37, 37, 40.5, 40.5, 42, 42) cm

C: 16" (40.5 cm)

D: 9¾ (9¾, 10, 10, 10, 10¾, 10¾)"
25 (25, 25.5, 25.5, 25.5, 27.5, 27.5) cm

E: 1½" (3.8 cm)

F: 3" (7.5 cm)

G: 13 (13, 13¼, 13¼, 13¼, 15¾, 15¾)"
33 (33, 33.5, 33.5, 33.5, 40, 40) cm

H: 11½ (11½, 12, 12, 12, 14, 14)"
29 (29, 30.5, 30.5, 30.5, 35.5, 35.5) cm

I: 9½ (9½, 11, 11, 11, 12½, 12½)"
24 (24, 28, 28, 28, 31.5, 31.5) cm

J: 13½ (13½, 14, 14, 14, 14½, 14½)"
34.5 (34.5, 25.5, 35.5, 35.5, 37, 37) cm

1½"
vertical
rise

shoulder

it surrounds. Sl m; pull the first stitch after the wraps snug so there is no gap and knit to beg-of-rnd m.

Knit to m, sl m, knit to first front short-row m. Remove m, k12 wrapped sts, picking up and knitting tbl each wrap with the stitch it surrounds. BO 54 (57, 60, 63, 67, 72, 75) sts to beg of rnd m, making sure to BO wrapped sts loosely.

Knit to m, then BO rem front sts, making sure to BO wrapped sts loosely. Break yarn, leaving an ample tail for weaving in.

BACK

You will now work the back as a single flat piece. Rejoin working yarn at the side that was your beg of rnd.

Row 1: (RS) Knit all sts, then, using the backward-loop cast-on, CO 18 sts. Turn.

Row 2: (WS) Purl all sts, then, using the backward loop cast-on, CO 18 sts. Turn.

Work back and forth in St st for 3½ (3½, 4, 4, 4, 5, 5)" (9 [9, 10, 10, 10, 12.5, 12.5] cm), ending having worked a WS row.

BACK SHAPING

Row 1: (RS) BO 18 sts, knit to end.

Row 2: (WS) BO 18 sts, purl to end.

Row 3: BO 16 (18, 19, 21, 23, 25, 27) sts, knit to end.

Row 4: BO 16 (18, 19, 21, 23, 25, 27) sts, purl to end.

Row 5: BO 17 (18, 20, 21, 23, 26, 27) sts, knit to end.

Row 6: BO 17 (18, 20, 21, 23, 26, 27) sts, purl to end.

ALTERNATING BRAIDED CABLE

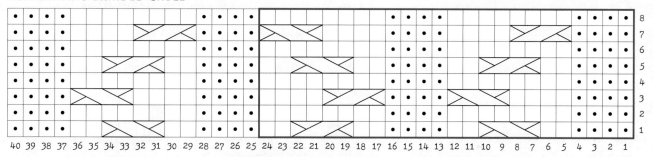

☐ knit on RS, purl on WS	⧗ 2/2RC
• purl on RS, knit on WS	☐ repeat
⧗ 2/2LC	

BO remaining 18 sts, placing rm on each side to mark the center bound-off section.

SHOULDER PANELS (MAKE 2)

Using longer cir, CO 78 (78, 80, 80, 80, 94, 94) sts.

Set-up row 1: (RS) K1, p6 (6, 7, 7, 7, 2, 2), pm, [p4, k8] 5 (5, 5, 5, 5, 7, 7) times, p4, pm, purl to last st, k1.

Set-up row 2: (WS) Knit the knit sts and purl the purl sts.

Begin Alternating Braided Cable patt. (see Stitch Guide or chart above)

⎸⎹⎸⎹⎸⎹⎸⎹⎸⎹⎸⎹⎸⎹⎸⎹⎸⎹⎸⎹⎸⎹⎸⎹⎸⎹⎸⎹⎸⎹⎸⎹⎸⎹⎸⎹⎸⎹

NOTE: *Stitch markers mark beg and end of Alternating Braided Cable patt. This piece is worked flat, so read even-numbered chart rows from left to right. Slip markers as you come to them.*

⎸⎹⎸⎹⎸⎹⎸⎹⎸⎹⎸⎹⎸⎹⎸⎹⎸⎹⎸⎹⎸⎹⎸⎹⎸⎹⎸⎹⎸⎹⎸⎹⎸⎹⎸⎹⎸⎹

Sizes – (– , 36, 38, 40¾, 44, 46)" (– [– , 91.5, 96.5, 103.5, 112, 117] cm) only

Set-up row 3: K1, purl to m, work Alternating Braided Cable to m, purl to last st, k1.

Set-up row 4: Knit the knit sts and purl the purl sts.

Repeat these two rows – (– , 7, 7, 7, 8, 8) more times.

All Sizes

Row 1: (RS) K1, purl to m, work Alternating Braided Cable to m, purl to last st, k1.

Row 2 and all WS rows: Knit the knit sts and purl the purl sts.

Row 3: Rep Row 1.

Row 5: (inc) K1, M1P, purl to m, work Alternating Braided Cable to m, purl to last st, M1P, k1—80 (80, 82, 82, 82, 96, 96) sts.

Rows 7–11: Rep Row 1.

Row 13: (inc) Rep Row 5—82 (82, 84, 84, 84, 98, 98) sts.

Sizes 32 (34, – , – , – , – , –)"
(81.5 [86.5, – , – , – , – , –] cm) only

Rows 15–45: Rep Rows 7–13 —90 sts.

Rows 47–73: Rep Row 1.

Row 74: Knit the knit sts and purl the purl sts.

BO all sts comfortably.

Sizes – (– , 36, 38, 40¾, – , –)" only

Rows 15–21: Rep Rows 7–13 —86 sts.

Row 23: Rep Row 1.

Row 25: K1, p5, k2, p3, work Alternating Braided Cable to m, p3, k2, p5, k1.

Row 27: K1, p4, k4, p2, work Alternating Braided Cable to m, p2, k4, p4, k1.

Row 29: (inc) K1, M1P, p3, k6, p1, work Alternating Braided Cable to m, p1, k6, p3, M1P, k1—88 sts.

Row 31: K1, p3, pm, k8, remove m, work Alternating Braided Cable to m, remove m, k8, pm, p3, k1.

Rows 33–35: Rep Row 1.

Row 37: (inc) Rep Row 5—90 sts.

Rows 39–53: Rep Rows 7–13 —94 sts.

Rows 55–71: Rep Row 1.

Row 72: Knit the knit sts and purl the purl sts.

BO all sts comfortably.

Sizes – (–, –, – , – , 44, 46)"
(– [–, – , – , – , 112, 117] cm) only

Rows 15–53: Rep Rows 7–13 —108 sts.

Rows 55–81: Rep Row 1.

Row 82: Knit the knit sts and purl the purl sts.

BO all sts comfortably.

PRE-ASSEMBLY BLOCKING

Wet-block the body and shoulder panel pieces to the measurements shown on the schematic. Steam-blocking will not achieve the desired results for this step. When blocking the body, make sure you accurately pin out the inverse V of the apex on the front panel and keep the shoulder seams angled on the back panel.

SEAMING SHOULDER PANELS

Position the shoulder panels so that the narrower ends form the bases of your sleeves and the wider ends form the V-neck of the sweater. In the back, seam each shoulder panel to the back piece from sleeve edge to neckline, which is marked on the back with a removable stitch marker. Stretch the back or sleeve panel as needed to match their lengths while seaming.

On the front piece, measure 1½" (3.8 cm) away from the tip of the inverted V on each side (along the edge of the V) and place removable markers at these points. Seam each shoulder panel to the front, from the sleeve edge to the removable marker, stretching the front or sleeve panel as needed to match their lengths. (The unseamed portions of the V will be joined with neck ribbing later.)

COLLAR

With RS facing, starting at rm on right front (at beg of right shoulder panel), pick up and knit sts across bound-off edge of right shoulder panel. (Do not pick up sts along the inverted V of the front body!) Pick up and knit about 1 st for every bound-off st in the purl sections of the shoulder panel and about 6 sts for every "cable column" —about 80 (80, 80, 80, 80, 94, 94) sts. Pick up and knit 14 sts along the back neck, then pick up and knit the same number of sts for the second shoulder panel as you did for the first—about 174 (174, 174, 174, 174, 202, 202) total sts.

Turn to work a WS row and purl to end.

Work flat in 2x2 ribbing for 1½" (3.8 cm)—about 12 rows.

BO comfortably in pattern. Seam the vertical edges of the collar ribbing to the inverted V of the center front, meeting them at the point.

SLEEVES (MAKE 2)

⊥⊥⊥⊥⊥⊥⊥⊥⊥⊥⊥⊥⊥⊥⊥⊥⊥⊥⊥⊥⊥⊥⊥⊥⊥⊥⊥⊥⊥⊥⊥⊥⊥⊥⊥⊥⊥⊥

NOTE: *This sweater is designed with bracelet-length sleeves that end right before the wristbone begins. If you would like to adjust the sleeve length, add eight rounds of Stockinette stitch for every 1" (2.5 cm) you want to add, after the decrease rounds are completed. The current length as written is 16" (40.5 cm) from underarm.*

⊥⊥⊥⊥⊥⊥⊥⊥⊥⊥⊥⊥⊥⊥⊥⊥⊥⊥⊥⊥⊥⊥⊥⊥⊥⊥⊥⊥⊥⊥⊥⊥⊥⊥⊥⊥⊥⊥

Starting at the underarm seam, pick up and knit about 78 (78, 80, 80, 80, 94, 94) sts around armhole. Pm and join for working in the round. Work in St st for 9 rnds.

Dec rnd: K3, k2tog, knit to last 5 sts, ssk, k3.

Work in St st and repeat Dec rnd every 9th rnd 9 more times—58 (58, 60, 60, 60, 74, 74) sts.

Work in 2x2 ribbing for 12 rnds.

BO in pattern comfortably.

FINISHING

Steam-block your finished sweater to relax the seams and lengthen the arms.

Soho SHAWL

The Soho Shawl was inspired by the wonderful yarn
that it's knit out of: Purl Soho's Super Soft Merino. The shawl
is a timeless piece that features an addictive, easy-to-memorize
pattern—perfect for a chatty coffee downtown! The finished piece
is the coziest and warmest woolly thing for the neck. Easy to wear
and quick to knit! — **MELODY HOFFMANN**

FINISHED SIZE
About 35½" (90 cm) wide
and 44½" (113 cm) long.

YARN
Bulky weight
(#6 super bulky).

Shown here: Purl Soho
Super Soft Merino
(100% Merino wool; 87 yd
[80 m]/3½ oz [100 g]):
rose granite, 6 skeins.

NEEDLES
Size U.S. 11 (8 mm).

*Adjust needle size if
necessary to obtain
the correct gauge.*

NOTIONS
Tapestry needle;
scissors (for tassels).

GAUGE
12 sts and 20 rows =
4" (10 cm) in st patt
after blocking.

Chart A

Row 1: (RS) K3, M1L, k2.

Row 2: (WS) K2, p2, k2.

Row 3: K3, p1, M1L, k2.

Row 4: K2, p1, k1, p1, k2.

Row 5: K5, M1L, k2.

Row 6: K2, p4, k2.

Row 7: K2, p4, M1L, k2.

Row 8: K2, p1, k6.

Row 9: K5, p1, k1, M1L, k2.

Row 10: K2, p2, k1, p3, k2.

Row 11: K2, p2, [k1, p1] twice, M1L, k2.

Row 12: K2, [p1, k1] twice, p1, k4.

Row 13: K3, p1, k1, p1, k3, M1L, k2.

Row 14: K2, p4, [k1, p1] twice, k2.

Row 15: K3, p1, k1, p5, M1L, k2.

Row 16: K2, p1, k5, p1, k1, p1, k2.

Row 17: K3, p1, k5, p1, k1, M1L, k2.

Row 18: K2, p2, k1, p5, k1, p1, k2.

Row 19: K3, p5, [k1, p1] twice, M1L, k2.

Row 20: K2, [p1, k1] twice, p1, k5, p1, k2.

Row 21: K7, p1, k1, p1, k3, M1L, k2.

Row 22: K2, p4, k1, p1, k1, p5, k2.

Row 23: K2, p4, k1, p1, k1, p5, M1L, k2.

Row 24: K2, p1, k5, p1, k1, p1, k6.

Row 25: K5, p1, k1, p1, k5, p1, k1, M1L, k2.

Row 26: K2, p2, k1, p5, k1, p1, k1, p3, k2.

Row 27: K2, p2, k1, p1, k1, p5, [k1, p1] twice, M1L, k2.

Row 28: K2, [p1, k1] twice, p1, k5, p1, k1, p1, k4.

Row 29: K3, p1, k1, p1, k5, p1, k1, p1, k3, M1L, k2.

Row 30: K2, p4, k1, p1, k1, p5, k1, p1, k1, p1, k2.

CHART B

Row 1: (RS) K2, *k1, p1, k1, p5; rep from * to last 2 sts, M1L, k2.

Row 2: (WS) K2, p1, *k5, p1, k1, p1; rep from * to last 2 sts, k2.

Row 3: K2, *k1, p1, k5, p1; rep from * to last 3 sts, k1, M1L, k2.

Row 4: K2, p2, *k1, p5, k1, p1; rep from * to last 2 sts, k2.

Row 5: K2, *k1, p5, k1, p1; rep from * to last 4 sts, k1, p1, M1L, k2.

Row 6: K2, p1, k1, p1, *k1, p1, k5, p1; rep from * to last 2 sts, k2.

Row 7: K2, *k5, p1, k1, p1; rep from * to last 5 sts, k3, M1L, k2.

Row 8: K2, p4, *k1, p1, k1, p5; rep from * to last 2 sts, k2.

Row 9: K2, *p4, [k1, p1] twice; rep from * to last 6 sts, p4, M1L, k2.

Row 10: K2, p1, k4, *[k1, p1] twice, k4; rep from * to last 2 sts, k2.

Row 11: K2, *k3, p1, k1, p1, k2; rep from * to last 7 sts, k3, p1, k1, M1L, k2.

Row 12: K2, p2, k1, p3, *p2, k1, p1, k1, p3; rep from * to last 2 sts, k2.

Row 13: K2, *p2, k1, p1, k1, p3; rep from * to last 8 sts, p2, k1, p1, k2, M1L, k2.

Row 14: K2, p3, k1, p1, k2, *k3, p1, k1, p1, k2; rep from * to last 2 sts, k2.

Row 15: K2, *[k1, p1] twice, k4; rep from * to last 9 sts, [k1, p1] twice, k3, M1L, k2.

Row 16: K2, p4, [k1, p1] twice, *p4, [k1, p1] twice; rep from * to last 2 sts, k2.

Instructions

CO 1 st.

Set-up row 1: (RS) K1f&b.

Set-up row 2: Knit to end.

Set-up row 3: Knit to last st, M1L, k1.

Set-up row 4: Knit to end.

Repeat Set-up rows 3 and 4 twice more—5 sts.

NOTE: *All wrong-side chart rows are worked as follows: Work the first and last two stitches in garter stitch (knit on all rows), then knit the knit stitches and purl the purl stitches in the body of the shawl. If you're not familiar with reading your knitting, you can follow the written instructions (see Stitch Guide) or the charts for the WS rows.*

Work Rows 1–30 of Chart A—20 sts.

Work Rows 1–16 of Chart B. Repeat Chart B until you have 103 sts, ending after a Row 5.

Next row: (WS) Knit to end.

Loosely BO all sts knitwise.

CHART A

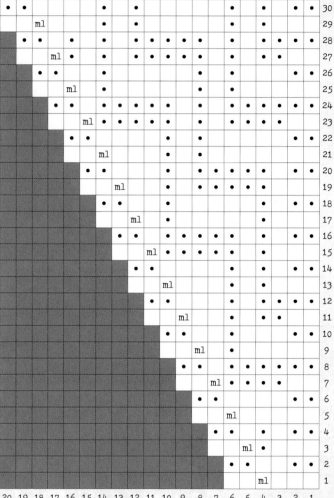

CHART B

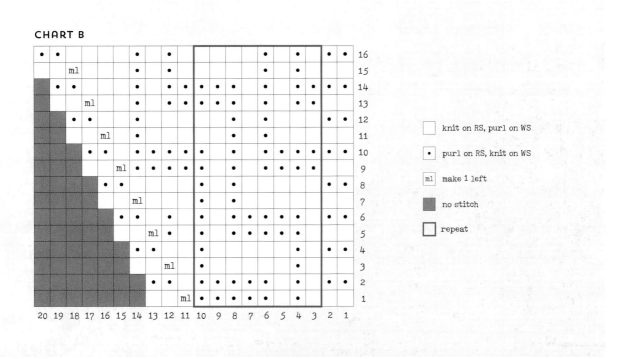

Column numbers (left to right): 20 19 18 17 16 15 14 13 12 11 10 9 8 7 6 5 4 3 2 1

Row numbers (bottom to top): 1–16

Legend:
- ☐ knit on RS, purl on WS
- • purl on RS, knit on WS
- ml make 1 left
- ▨ no stitch
- ☐ repeat

FINISHING

Weave in ends and block
to measurements.

Make 3 tassels (see Techniques) and
attach one at each corner of shawl.

35½" (90 cm)

direction
of work

44½" (113 cm)

Twirling SOCKS

A project to bring to knit group gatherings should be portable, and the pattern should be easy to memorize so that one doesn't lose track while chatting. These socks meet those criteria perfectly. The main pattern is a knit-and-purl ribbing, which travels to the side every couple of rounds. The interesting detail is the heel because the heel flap and gusset are integrated into the leg and are worked in the round. The skewed heel flap "triangle" emerges from one of the knit columns in the ribbing. — **MONE DRÄGER**

FINISHED SIZE
About 6¼ (7½, 8½)" (16 [19, 21.5] cm) leg circumference. Leg length and foot length are adjustable.

Project shown measures 7½" (19 cm).

YARN
Fingering weight (#1 superfine).

Shown here: Sweet Georgia Yarns Tough Love Sock (80% superwash Merino wool, 20% nylon; 425 yd (388 m)/4 oz [115 g]): jasmine, 1 skein.

NEEDLES
Size U.S. 1 (2.25 mm).

Adjust needle size if necessary to obtain the correct gauge.

NOTIONS
2 stitch markers (m), 1 removable (rm); tapestry needle.

GAUGE
32 sts and 42 rnds = 4" (10 cm) in Stockinette st after blocking.

NOTES
— These socks are worked in the round from the cuff down. They are mirror images of each other, with the stripes and the heel flap slanting in different directions with individual instructions for each sock. The pattern "travels" around the leg of the sock. Every fourth round of the leg you will move one stitch to the beginning of the next round or the end of the previous round to establish the new beginning of the round. Due to the "travel" of the pattern you will have to move stitches between needles.

— The increases for the heel are worked into the first knit stripe of the pattern at the beginning of the round. All increases are made using lifted increases.

Instructions

RIGHT SOCK

LEG

CO 50 (60, 70) sts, pm and join for working in the round, being careful not to twist. *Work Rnds 1–4 of Right Leg Chart, repeating chart 10 (12, 14) times around leg.

Shift beg of rnd: Remove m, k1, pm for new beg of rnd.

Rep from * 14 (15, 16) more times, or to desired length to top of heel. Rep Rnds 1 and 2 of Right Leg Chart once more.

HEEL

The increases for the heel flap are worked into the first knit stripe of the round. Use the last knit stitch of this stripe for the lifted increase. Keep all other sts in leg pattern and continue as established, including the shift of the beg of rnd and the travel of the pattern after 4 rounds.

Rnd 1: K2, rli, k1, p2; work to end in established patt—1 st inc'd.

Rnd 2: Knit to last knit st in first stripe, rli, k1, p2, work to end in patt—1 st inc'd.

Rep last rnd 24 (28, 32) more times —29 (33, 37) knit sts in the first stripe, 76 (90, 104) sts total. Remove m.

TURN HEEL

The heel will be turned in short-rows; keep remaining sts on hold for instep.

Short-row 1: (RS) K6, ssk, k1, turn.

Short-row 2: (WS) Sl1 wyf, p6 (7, 8), p2tog, p1, turn.

Short-row 3: Sl1 wyb, knit to 1 st before gap, ssk, k1, turn.

Short-row 4: Sl1 wyf, purl to 1 st before gap, p2tog, p1, turn.

Rep Short-rows 3 and 4 seven (nine, eleven) more times—58 (68, 78) sts.

Next row: Sl1 wyb, knit to 1 st before gap, ssk, turn.

Next row: Sl1 wyf, purl to 1 st before gap, p2tog, turn.

Rep last 2 rows 2 more times —52 (62, 72) sts.

FOOT

Set-up row: Sl1 wyb, knit to 1 st before gap, ssk, pm for new beg of rnd—51 (61, 71) sts.

Rnd 1: Work Right Instep Chart across 25 (30, 35) instep sts, pm, k2tog, knit to end—50 (60, 70) sts.

Next rnd: Work Right Instep Chart to m, knit to end.

Rep last rnd, repeating Rnds 1–20 of Right Instep Chart as needed, until foot measures about 1½ (2¼, 2¾)" (3.8 [5.5, 7] cm) less than desired length.

TOE

Size 6¼" (16 cm) only
Set-up rnd: *K11, ssk, k12; rep from * once mor—48 sts.

Size 7½" (19 cm) only
Set-up rnd: *Ssk, k13; rep from * 3 more times—56 sts.

Size 8½" (21.5 cm) only
Set-up rnd: *K8, [ssk, k7] 3 times; rep from * once more—64 sts.

All sizes
Knit 2 rnds.

Dec rnd: *Ssk, k4 (5, 6); rep from * to end—40 (48, 56) sts.

Knit 4 (5, 6) rnds.

Dec rnd: *Ssk, k3 (4, 5); rep from * to end—32 (40, 48) sts.

Knit 3 (4, 5) rnds.

Dec rnd: *Ssk, k2 (3, 4); rep from * to end—24 (32, 40) sts.

Knit 2 (3, 4) rnds.

Dec rnd: *Ssk, k1 (2, 3); rep from * to end—16 (24, 32) sts.

Knit 1 (2, 3) rnd(s).

Sizes 7½" and 8½" (19 and 21.5 cm) only
Dec rnd: *Ssk, k1 (2); rep from * to end—16 (24) sts.

Knit 1 (2) rnd(s).

Size 8½" (21.5 cm) only
Dec rnd: *Ssk, k1; rep from * to end—16 sts.

Knit 1 rnd.

All sizes
Dec rnd: Ssk to end—8 sts.

Break yarn and draw tail through rem sts. Pull tight to gather sts and fasten off on WS.

RIGHT LEG

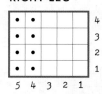

LEFT LEG

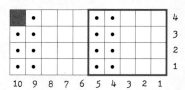

RIGHT INSTEP

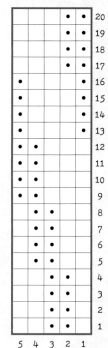

LEFT INSTEP

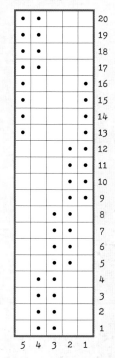

☐ knit

• purl

☐ work 5 (6, 7) times

☐ work 9 (11, 13) times

☐ work 10 (12, 14) times

■ no stitch, rnd ends 1 st early

LEFT SOCK

LEG
CO 50 (60, 70) sts, prm and join for working in the round, being careful not to twist. *Work Rnds 1–4 of Left Leg Chart.

NOTE: *Rnd 4 ends one st before beg-of-rnd m. Remove rm and prm (after working just one purl st) for new beg of rnd.*

Rep from * 14 (15, 16) more times, or to desired length to top of heel. Rep Rnds 1 and 2 of Left Leg Chart once more.

HEEL

The increases for the heel flap are worked into the first knit stripe of the round. Use the first knit stitch of this stripe for the lifted increase. Keep all other stitches in leg pattern and continue as established, including the shift of the beg of rnd and the travel of the pattern after 4 rounds.

Rnd 1: K1, lli, k2, p2, work to end in established patt—1 st inc'd.

Rnd 2: K1, lli, work to end in patt—1 st inc'd.

Rep last rnd 24 (28, 32) more times —29 (33, 37) knit sts in the first stripe, 76 (90, 104) sts total. Remove rm.

TURN HEEL

The heel will be turned in short-rows over the first 51 (60, 69) sts of the rnd; keep remaining sts on hold for instep.

Short-row 1: (RS) K28 (33, 38), ssk, k1, turn.

Finish heel turn as for right sock, starting with Short-row 2.

FOOT

Work as for right sock, using Left Instep Chart.

TOE

Size 6¼" (16 cm) only

Set-up rnd: *K12, k2tog, k11; rep from * once more—48 sts.

Size 7½" (19 cm) only

Set-up rnd: *K13, k2tog; rep from * 3 more times—56 sts.

Size 8½" (21.5 cm) only

Set-up rnd: *[K7, k2tog] 3 times, k8; rep from * once more—64 sts.

All sizes

Knit 2 rnds.

Dec rnd: *K4 (5, 6), k2tog; rep from * to end—40 (48, 56) sts.

Knit 4 (5, 6) rnds.

Dec rnd: *K3 (4, 5), k2tog; rep from * to end—32 (40, 48) sts.

Knit 3 (4, 5) rnds.

Dec rnd: *K2 (3, 4), k2tog; rep from * to end—24 (32, 40) sts.

Knit 2 (3, 4) rnds.

Dec rnd: *K1 (2, 3), k2tog; rep from * to end—16 (24, 32) sts.

Knit 1 (2, 3) rnd(s).

Sizes 7½" and 8½" (19 and 21.5 cm) only

Dec rnd: *K1 (2), k2tog; rep from * to end—16 (24) sts.

Knit 1 (2) rnd(s).

Size 8½" (21.5 cm) only

Dec rnd: *K1, k2tog; rep from * to end—16 sts.

Knit 1 rnd.

All sizes

Dec rnd: K2tog to end—8 sts.

Break yarn and draw tail through rem sts. Pull tight to gather sts and fasten off on WS.

FINISHING

Weave in ends. Block.

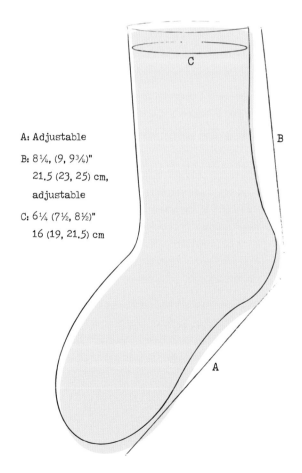

A: Adjustable

B: 8¼, (9, 9¾)"
   21.5 (23, 25) cm,
   adjustable

C: 6¼ (7½, 8½)"
   16 (19, 21.5) cm

BETTER TOGETHER: THE KNITTING COMMUNITY & ME

by Maya Elson

I STARTED OUT KNITTING solo. Though the ability to do it was planted by my grandmother, I didn't really embrace it as a child. That came later, without companion or teacher. It was just me and the yarn and needles, on a mission of sorts.

Mine is not an especially unique story: girl graduates from college, starts first job, is disappointed by the realities of becoming a grown-up. Girl ponders the meaning of life. Girl takes up knitting.

One day I was in Urban Outfitters, of all places, browsing the sales racks, and I noticed a knitting book on a display table. Whether it was the familiar pull of a craft I vaguely knew I could do, or the surprise of seeing a knitting book in Urban Outfitters, I picked it up and thumbed through. A 2x2 ribbed scarf caught my eye. I studied the photo and instructions and became convinced that I didn't need this book to knit that scarf. I could do it all by myself.

One trip to a big-box craft store later, I was off and knitting. My grandmother's lessons must have been good, because I remembered enough to cast on and knit, just like that. Thinking I should practice my knits and purls before I attempted my first scarf, I started with some red acrylic yarn and kept knitting until I ran out. Despite my sore fingertips and tired wrists, I persisted. It wasn't long before I had churned out a tightly knit white acrylic 2x2 ribbed scarf.

As I continued to wrestle with questions about life and work and what it all was for, I turned ever more to knitting: scarf after scarf, then a poncho, an acrylic bouclé sweater, and, curiously, pants. Most of these items were kind of terrible and unwearable, but all that mattered to me at the time was creating stitches that turned into something concrete.

To be honest, the negative (and incorrect) social narrative of knitting being stodgy, unhip, and for old ladies must have in some part gotten to me. Because at first I was rather secretive about what I was knitting… and the fact I was doing it at all. But as passions often do, it wanted to come out. I tested the waters with friends, expressing the transformative powers knitting could have over yarn, and over me. Instead of a light jacket, I cautiously stepped out in my voluminous, handknit, Stevie Nicks–channeling poncho.

Eventually, I taught a few friends to knit. They invited others along and I taught them, too. Before long we had a standing knit night, and knitting became so much more to me than a craft that could help me cope with an existential crisis.

One could say knitting is technically an individual sport. It's all for one and one for all—the "all" being the knitting and the "one" being the knitter. It's not something you need other people to do. You can learn it from a book, shop for supplies online, and go for it completely, 100% alone.

And yet, knitters seem to inevitably come together. We connect over the fact that we persist with—and love—this craft that no longer has the same necessity and practical application it once did. We bond over the fact that even though we could buy a sweater for half the price in a fraction of the time compared to knitting one, we knit that sweater anyway! We help each other break away from knitting unwearable, frankly ugly items to create beautiful knits. It's gratifying to have others involved in the knitting process who just "get it." Their encouragement and their "oohs" and "ahhs" over your finished objects come from a place of understanding that you can't get from anyone else.

One thing that I never expected as I entered this community is how broad it is, and what this breadth can bring out in a knitter. Because it isn't just knitters; it is also knitwear designers, yarn manufacturers, spinners, dyers, farmers, yarn shop owners… and the list goes on. While I started out focused on knitting and purling as a distraction, I'm now also invested in the organizations and individuals who contribute to making knitting what it is today. We can support small businesses by shopping at local yarn stores. Buying yarn directly from independent dyers supports one person's art in a meaningful way. By taking time to learn about where wool comes from and choosing yarn that supports small farms, we play a small part in sustainability. All of this trickles down to keeping knitting an interesting, vibrant, exciting craft and community.

Almost 20 years since that day in Urban Outfitters, I've found myself part of something truly special. I wasn't looking for it, not at first. It wasn't necessarily looking for me. But there was space for me. And there's space for anyone so inclined to wield sticks and string. So go ahead, knit in public. Talk about new pattern releases and yarn lines as you might discuss celebrity gossip. Go to fiber festivals and buy handspun yarn from hidden-gem sheep farms. Or simply use your knitting as an excellent excuse to get together with your knitting friends for some good coffee talk. Because knitting is good on its own, but it's even better together with friends. —

Cremoso SHAWL

Cremoso is a semicircular asymmetrical shawl, featuring unusual decreases and an irregularly shaped lace edging. It's a fun knit and, despite the lace being worked on both sides, it's rather simple and easily memorized. *Cremoso* means creamy in Italian and indicates how any espresso should be: a creamy shot of instant bliss! — **SARA MATERNINI**

\|\|\|\|\|\|\|\|\|\|\|\|\|\|\|\|\|\|\|\|\|\|\|\|\|\|\|\|\|\|\|\|\|\|\|\|\|\|\|\|\|

FINISHED SIZE
About 72" (183 cm) wide and 35" (89 cm) deep.

YARN
Fingering weight (#1 superfine).

Shown here: Hazel Knits Artisan Sock (90% superwash Merino wool, 10% nylon; 400 yd [366 m]/4¼ oz [120 g]): acorn, 3 skeins.

NEEDLES
Size U.S. 4 (3.5 mm).

Size U.S. 6 (4 mm) for bind-off.

Adjust needle size if necessary to obtain the correct gauge.

NOTIONS
4 stitch markers (m) of different colors; tapestry needle; blocking pins; flexible blocking wires (optional).

GAUGE
22 sts and 32 rows = 4" (10 cm) in Stockinette st with smaller needles after blocking.

NOTE
— Take the time to learn how to slip two stitches together purlwise through the back loop (the slipped sts in the wrong-side decrease pcdd); it's a bit difficult at first, but the final result is worth the effort.

cdd: Slip 2 stitches together knitwise, knit 1, pass slipped stitches over.

pcdd: Slip 2 stitches together purlwise through the back loop as if to p2tog tbl; purl 1, pass slipped stitches over.

Lace Chart A

Row 1: (RS) *Yo, k2, cdd, k2, yo, k7.

Row 2: (WS) *P8, yo, p1, pcdd, p1, yo, p1.

Row 3: *K2, yo, cdd, yo, k9.

Row 4: *Yo, p2, pcdd, p2, yo, p7.

Row 5: *K8, yo, k1, cdd, k1, yo, k1.

Row 6: *P2, yo, pcdd, yo, p9.

Lace Chart B

Row 1: (RS) *Yo, k2, cdd, k2, yo, k7; rep from * to last 7 sts, yo, k2, cdd, k2, yo.

Row 2: (WS) P1, yo, p1, pcdd, p1, yo, p1, *p8, yo, p1, pcdd, p1, yo, p1; rep from * to end.

Row 3: *K2, yo, cdd, yo, k9; rep from * to last 7 sts, k2, yo, cdd, yo, k2.

Row 4: P7, *yo, p2, pcdd, p2, yo, p7; rep from * to end.

Row 5: *K8, yo, k1, cdd, k1, yo, k1; rep from * to last 7 sts, k7.

Row 6: P7, *p2, yo, pcdd, yo, p9; rep from * to end.

Lace Chart C

Row 1: (WS) P7, yo, p2, pcdd, p2, yo.

Row 2: (RS) K1, yo, k1, cdd, k1, yo, k8.

Row 3: P9, yo, pcdd, yo, p2.

Row 4: K7, yo, k2, cdd, k2, yo.

Row 5: P1, yo, p1, pcdd, p1, yo, p8.

Row 6: K9, yo, cdd, yo, k2.

Instructions

GARTER TAB CAST-ON

With smaller needle, CO 3 sts.

Knit 6 rows. Do not turn work after the final row.

Rotate the work 90 degrees and pick up and knit 3 sts down the long side edge, picking up from each well in the garter st—6 sts.

Rotate the work 90 degrees and pick up and knit 3 sts along the cast-on edge—9 sts. Turn work.

INCREASE ROWS

Row 1 and all other WS rows: K3, purl to last 3 sts, k2, sl1 wyf.

Row 2: (RS) K3, yo, knit to last 3 sts, yo, k2, sl1 wyf—11 sts.

Row 4: K3, yo, k1, yo, pm, k1, yo, k1, yo, pm, k1, yo, k1, yo, k2, sl1 wyf—17 sts.

Row 6: K3, yo, knit to m, yo, sl m, k1, yo, knit to last st, sl1 wyf—3 sts inc'd.

Row 8: K3, yo, *knit to m, yo, sl m, k1, yo; rep from * once, knit to last 3 sts, yo, k2, sl1 wyf—6 sts inc'd.

Row 9: K3, purl to last 3 sts, k2, sl1 wyf.

Repeat Rows 6–9 until you have 317 sts, ending after a Row 7.

Row 140: K3, yo, knit to m, yo, sl m, k1, yo, knit to last 3 sts, yo, k2, sl1 wyf—321 sts.

Row 141: K3, purl to last 3 sts, k2, sl1 wyf—142 sts from BOR to first m; 105 sts from first m to second m; 74 sts from second m to end.

Row 142: (RS) K3, yo, knit to 3 sts before m, pm; work Row 1 of Chart A 8 times, removing next m when you come to it; pm, knit to last st, removing last m when you come to it, sl1 wyf—322 sts.

Row 143: (WS) K3, purl to m, work next row of Chart A to m, purl to last 3 sts, k2, sl1 wyf.

Row 144: K3, yo, knit to m, work Chart A to m, knit to last 3 sts, yo, k2, sl1 wyf—324 sts.

Row 145: Rep Row 143.

Row 146: K3, yo, knit to m, work Chart A to m, knit to last st, sl1 wyf—325 sts.

Row 147: Rep Row 143.

Row 148: K3, yo, knit to 14 sts before m, pm, *work Row 1 of Chart A to m, remove m; rep from * once more, work one more chart repeat, pm, knit to last 3 sts, yo, k2, sl1 wyf—327 sts.

Row 149: Rep Row 143.

Row 150: K3, yo, knit to m, work Chart A to m, knit to last st, sl1 wyf—328 sts.

Row 151: Rep Row 143.

Row 152: K3, yo, knit to m, work Chart A to m, knit to last 3 sts, yo, k2, sl1 wyf—330 sts.

Row 153: Rep Row 143.

Row 154: K3, yo, knit to 14 sts before m, pm, *work Row 1 of Chart A to m, remove m; rep from * once more, work one more chart repeat, pm, knit to last st, sl1 wyf—331 sts.

Row 155: Rep Row 143.

Row 156: K3, yo, knit to m, work Chart A to m, knit to last 3 sts, yo, k2, sl1 wyf—333 sts.

Row 157: Rep Row 143.

Row 158: K3, yo, knit to m, work Chart A to m, knit to last st, sl1 wyf—334 sts.

Row 159: Rep Row 143.

Rep Rows 148–159 once more —343 sts.

Rep Rows 148 and 149 once more —345 sts.

Row 174: (RS) K3, yo, knit to m, work Chart A to m, knit to last 3 sts, yo, k2, sl1 wyf —347 sts.

Row 175: (WS) Rep Row 143.

Row 176: Rep Row 174 —349 sts, 10 sts from last m to end.

Row 177: Rep Row 143.

Row 178: K3, yo, knit to 28 sts before m, pm, work Row 1 of Chart B to last 3 sts, removing markers as you come to them, k2, sl1 wyf —350 sts.

Row 179: K3, work Chart B to m, purl to last 2 sts, k2, sl1 wyf.

Row 180: K3, yo, knit to m, work Chart B to last 3 sts, k2, sl1 wyf —351 sts.

Row 181: Rep Row 179.

Row 182: Rep Row 180 —352 sts.

Row 183: Rep Row 179.

Rep Rows 178–183 once more —355 sts.

Remove all markers.

Row 190: (RS) K3, yo, k6, work Row 1 of Chart B to last 3 sts, k2, sl1 wyf —356 sts.

Row 191: (WS) K3, work Row 2 of Chart B to last 10 sts, p7, k2, sl1 wyf.

Row 192: K10, work Row 3 of Chart B to last 3 sts, k2, sl1 wyf.

CHART A

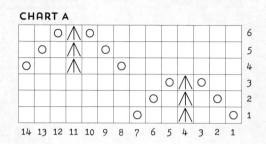

14 13 12 11 10 9 8 7 6 5 4 3 2 1

CHART B

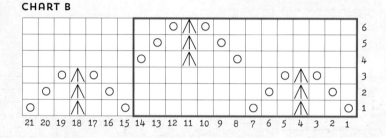

21 20 19 18 17 16 15 14 13 12 11 10 9 8 7 6 5 4 3 2 1

CHART C

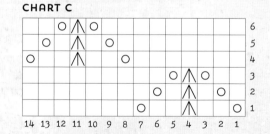

14 13 12 11 10 9 8 7 6 5 4 3 2 1

Row 1 is a WS row and should be read from left to right

☐ knit on RS, purl on WS   ⊙ yo

⋀ cdd on RS, pcdd on WS   ☐ repeat

Row 193: K3, work Row 1 of Chart C to last 3 sts, k2, sl1 wyf.

|||||||||||||||||||||||||||||||||||||||||||||||||||||

NOTE: *The charted versions of Chart A and Chart C are identical; but because Chart C starts with a WS row (while Chart A starts with a RS row), the written instructions are different.*

|||||||||||||||||||||||||||||||||||||||||||||||||||||

Rows 194–198: K3, work next row of Chart C to last 3 sts, k2, sl1 wyf.

Rep Rows 193–198 three more times—356 sts.

BIND-OFF

With larger needle, BO all sts as follows:

*P2tog, put st just formed back on left needle; rep from * until 1 st remains.

Break yarn and pull tail through last loop.

FINISHING

Wet-block to measurements, being careful to let the lace bloom. On the border, pin out all the points. Weave in ends.

Morning Brew
SWEATER

This simple boxy sweater is intended to be comfortable but not overly slouchy. It's knit in a beautiful yarn, with a unique mesh lace V-neck detail. Once you put it on, you won't want to take it off—wear it to work, to the basketball game, or even better, to knit night. — **KIRI FITZGERALD**

〬〬〬〬〬〬〬〬〬〬〬〬〬〬〬〬〬〬〬〬〬〬〬

FINISHED SIZE

About 36 (40, 44, 48, 52)" (91.5 [101.5, 112, 122, 132] cm).

Garment shown measures 40" (102 cm), modeled with 6" (15 cm) of ease.

YARN

DK weight (#3 light).

Shown here: Skein Voyage (100% superwash Merino wool; 230 yd [210 m]/3½ oz [100 g]): slate, 5 (5, 6, 6, 7) skeins.

NEEDLES

Size U.S. 6 (4 mm): 32" (80 cm) circular (cir),
16" (40 cm) cir, and double-pointed (dpn).

Size U.S. 5 (3.75 mm): 32" (80 cm) cir and dpn.

Adjust needle size if necessary to obtain the correct gauge.

NOTIONS

2 stitch markers (m); 1 removable stitch marker (rm) or safety pin; stitch holders or waste yarn; tapestry needle.

GAUGE

20 sts and 27 rnds = 4" (10 cm) in Stockinette st on larger needle after blocking.

NOTES

— Back yoke is 1½ (1½, 1¼, 1, ¾)" (3.8 [3.8, 3.2, 2.5, 2] cm) shorter than the front at arm opening; this is deliberate and causes the shoulder seam to fall at the back of the shoulder.

— When working neckband across back neck and down left-hand side, keep stitches firm to avoid a loose lifted stitch. When working neckband up right-hand side, keep stitches loose to avoid over-tightening the lifted stitch; the yarnover is worked before the lifted stitch to help avoid this.

Instructions

Using smaller 32" (81.5 cm) cir needle, CO 180 (200, 220, 240, 260) sts, pm and join for working in the round, being careful not to twist.

Work in [k2, p2] rib for 2" (5 cm).

Switch to larger cir needle and work in St st until piece measures 16" (40.5 cm) from cast-on.

SPLIT FOR V-NECK

Row 1: (RS) K43 (48, 53, 58, 63), place next 2 sts on rm, turn work—178 (198, 218, 238, 258) sts left on neede.

Row 2: (WS) Purl to m, p90 (100, 110, 120, 130), pm, purl to sts placed on rm—end of row.

Row 3: K2, ssk, knit to last 4 sts, k2tog, k2—2 sts dec'd.

Row 4: Purl to end.

Rep last 2 rows 6 more times —164 (184, 204, 224, 244) sts.

SPLIT FOR UNDERARMS

K2, ssk, knit to m, turn work—35 (40, 45, 50, 55) sts for right front. Place 90 (100, 110, 120, 130) back sts and 36 (41, 46, 51, 56) left front sts on stitch holders.

RIGHT FRONT

Row 1: (WS) Purl to end.

Row 2: K2, ssk, knit to end—1 st dec'd.

Rep last 2 rows 11 (12, 12, 13, 13) more times—23 (27, 32, 36, 41) sts.

Work even in St st until piece measures 6 (6¼, 7, 7¾, 8½)" (15 [16, 18, 19.5, 21.5] cm) from underarm split, ending with a WS row.

SHOULDER SHAPING

Short-row 1: (RS) Knit to last 4 (5, 6, 7, 8) sts, w&t.

Short-row 2: (WS) Purl to end.

Short-row 3: Knit to 4 (5, 6, 7, 8) sts before wrapped st, w&t.

Short-row 4: Purl to end.

Rep last 2 rows 2 more times.

Row 9: Knit to end, working wraps together with their wrapped sts.

Work 3 rows even in St st, then break yarn, leaving a 9" (23 cm) tail. Place sts on holder.

LEFT FRONT

Return 36 (41, 46, 51, 56) left front sts to larger needle and join yarn ready to work a RS row.

Row 1: (RS) Knit to last 4 sts, k2tog, k2—1 st dec'd.

Row 2: Purl to end.

Rep last 2 rows 12 (13, 13, 14, 14) more times—23 (27, 32, 36, 41) sts.

Work even in St st until piece measures 6 (6¼, 7, 7¾, 8½)" (15 [16, 18, 19.5, 21.5] cm) from underarm split, ending with a WS row.

SHOULDER SHAPING

Rows 1 and 3: Knit to end.

Short-row 2: Purl to last 4 (5, 6, 7, 8) sts, w&t.

Short-row 4: Purl to 4 (5, 6, 7, 8) sts before wrapped st, w&t.

Short-row 5: Knit to end.

Rep last 2 rows 2 more times.

Row 10: Purl to end, working wraps together with their wrapped sts.

Row 11: Knit to end.

Break yarn, leaving a 9" (23 cm) tail. Place sts on holder.

BACK

Return 90 (100, 110, 120, 130) back sts to larger needle and join yarn ready to work a RS row.

Work even in St st until piece measures 4½ (4¾, 5¾, 6¾, 7¾)" (11.5 [12, 14.5, 17, 19.5] cm) from underarm split.

SHOULDER SHAPING

Short-row 1: (RS) Knit to last 4 (5, 6, 7, 8) sts, w&t.

Short-row 2: Purl to last 4 (5, 6, 7, 8) sts, w&t.

Short-row 3: Knit to 4 (5, 6, 7, 8) sts before wrapped st, w&t.

Short-row 4: Purl to 4 (5, 6, 7, 8) sts before wrapped st, w&t.

Rep last 2 rows 2 more times.

Short-row 9: Knit to end, working wraps together with their wrapped sts.

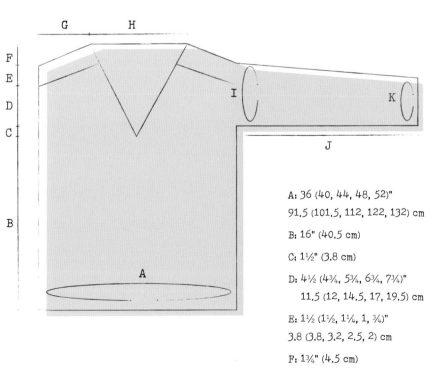

A: 36 (40, 44, 48, 52)"
91.5 (101.5, 112, 122, 132) cm

B: 16" (40.5 cm)

C: 1½" (3.8 cm)

D: 4½ (4¾, 5¾, 6¾, 7¾)"
11.5 (12, 14.5, 17, 19.5) cm

E: 1½ (1½, 1¼, 1, ¾)"
3.8 (3.8, 3.2, 2.5, 2) cm

F: 1¾" (4.5 cm)

G: 4½ (5½, 6½, 7¼, 8¼)"
11.5 (14, 16.5, 18.5, 21) cm

H: 8¾ (9¼, 9¼, 9½, 9½)"
22 (23.5, 23.5, 24, 24) cm

I: 11½ (12½, 14½, 16½, 18½)"
29 (31.5, 37, 42, 47) cm

J: 16½" (42 cm)

K: 8¾ (9½, 9½, 10½, 10½)"
22 (24, 24, 26.5, 26.5) cm

Row 10: Purl to end, working wraps together with their wrapped sts.

Row 11: Knit to end.

Row 12: P23 (27, 32, 36, 41).
Do not break yarn.

Join front and back shoulders (23 [27, 32, 36, 41] sts for each shoulder) using three-needle bind-off (see Techniques).

RIGHT SLEEVE

Using larger dpn, starting at underarm, pick up and knit 26 (28, 34, 38, 44) sts up back to shoulder seam, pick up and knit 32 (34, 38, 44, 48) sts down front to underarm, pm and join for working in the round—58 (62, 72, 82, 92) sleeve sts.

Knit 1 rnd.

Dec rnd: K2, k2tog, knit to 4 sts before m, ssk, k2—2 sts dec'd.

Rep Dec rnd every 12th (12th, 8th, 6th, 4th) rnd 6 (6, 11, 14, 19) more times—44 (48, 48, 52, 52) sts.

Work even in St st until sleeve measures 14½" (37 cm) from underarm.

Switch to smaller dpn and work in [k2, p2] rib for 2" (5 cm). Break yarn.

LEFT SLEEVE

Using larger dpn, starting at underarm, pick up and knit 32 (34, 38, 44, 48) sts up front to shoulder seam, pick up and knit 26 (28, 34, 38, 44) sts down back to underarm, pm and join for working in the round—58 (62, 72, 82, 92) sleeve sts.

Continue working as for right sleeve.

NECKLINE

Using larger 16" (40 cm) cir needle and with working yarn attached at back neck, knit across 44 (46, 46, 48, 48) back neck sts, pick up and knit 50 (54, 57, 61, 64) sts down left front, pm, k2 from rm, pick up and knit 51 (54, 57, 60, 63) sts up right front, pm and join for working in the rnd—147 (156, 162, 171, 177) sts.

Rnd 1: K2tog, knit to m, remove m, k2tog and mark this stitch with rm, knit to end—145 (154, 160, 169, 175) sts.

Rnd 2: *K3, with left needle lift first of the 3 sts just knit over the last 2 and off right needle, yo; rep from * to 3 sts before marked st, k2, cdd, move rm up 1 rnd (into center st just formed), k2, **yo, k3, sl3 sts back to left needle, with right needle lift 3rd st on left needle over first 2, sl2 sts back to right needle; rep from ** to end—143 (152, 158, 167, 173) sts.

Rnd 3 and all odd rnds: Knit to 1 st before marked st, cdd, move rm up 1 rnd, knit to end—2 sts dec'd.

Rnd 4: K1, *yo, k3, with left needle lift first of the 3 sts just knit over the last 2; rep from * to 3 sts before marked st, k2, cdd, move rm up 1 rnd, k2, **k3, sl3 sts back to left needle, with right needle lift 3rd st on left needle over first 2, sl2 sts back to right needle, yo; rep from ** to last st, k1—139 (148, 154, 163, 169) sts.

Rnd 6: *K3, with left needle lift first of the 3 sts just knit over the last 2, yo; rep from * to 2 sts before marked st, k1, cdd, move rm up 1 rnd, k1, **yo, k3, sl 3 sts back to left needle, with right needle lift 3rd st on left needle over first 2, sl 2 sts back to right needle; rep from ** to end—135 (144, 150, 159, 165) sts.

Rnd 8: K1, *yo, k3, with left needle lift first of the 3 sts just knit over the last 2; rep from * to 2 sts before marked st, k1, cdd, move rm up 1 rnd, k1, **k3, sl 3 sts back to left needle, with right needle lift 3rd st on left needle over first 2, sl 3 sts back to right needle, yo; rep from ** to last st, k1—131 (140, 146, 155, 161) sts.

Rnd 10: *K3, with left needle lift first of the 3 sts just knit over the last 2, yo; rep from * to 1 st before marked st, cdd, move rm up 1 rnd, **yo, k3, sl 3 sts back to left needle, with right needle lift 3rd st on left needle over first 2, sl 2 sts back to right needle; rep from ** to end—127 (136, 142, 151, 157) sts.

Rnd 12: K1, *yo, k3, with left needle lift first of the 3 sts just knit over the last 2; rep from * to 1 st before marked st, cdd, move rm up 1 rnd, **k3, sl 3 sts back to left needle, with right needle lift 3rd st on left needle over first 2, sl 2 sts back to right needle, yo; rep from ** to last st, k1—123 (132, 138, 147, 153) sts.

Rnd 13: Knit to 1 st before marked st, cdd, knit to end—121 (130, 136, 145, 151) sts.

With larger dpn, CO 2 sts onto left needle using the knitted cast-on. BO all neckline sts using the I-cord bind-off (see Techniques). BO 2 I-cord sts.

FINISHING

Weave in ends. Block to finished measurements.

BREAKFAST BRIOCHE *Scarf*

Brioche fabric is satisfying to knit as it works up into a squishy and plush ribbing. This scarf makes the brioche a little more interesting to knit by working it diagonally. Stitches are increased and/or decreased at each edge of the scarf on every fourth row; otherwise it's the same basic brioche ribbing that is so well loved by many a knitter. — **KRISTEN TENDYKE**

FINISHED SIZE
About 5" (12.5 cm) wide, and 60" (152.5 cm) long.

YARN
DK weight (#3 light).

Shown here: Bumblebirch Quill (100% superwash Merino wool; 231 yd [211 m]/3½ oz [100 g]): puddle, 2 skeins.

NEEDLES
Size U.S. 8 (5 mm).

Adjust needle size if necessary to obtain the correct gauge.

NOTIONS
Removable stitch marker (rm); tapestry needle.

GAUGE
18 sts and 21 brioche rows = 4" (10 cm) in Brioche Ribbing (see Notes) after blocking.

NOTES
— Because of the slipped stitches in the Brioche Ribbing pattern, when counting rows in the Brioche Ribbing, each row that you see is actually two rows worked. The number of rows given in the gauge is what you'll see when counting the rows.

— Always knit the last stitch on every right-side row through the back loop, so the slipped selvedge stitch is not twisted.

— If using a hand-dyed yarn for this scarf, you may want to alternate skeins every fourth row to avoid color pooling and obvious color changes between skeins. I suggest doing this on the row following an increase or decrease row by working as follows: Drop the old yarn over the new yarn, then pick up the new yarn. Slip the first st purlwise wyb, then work the row as instructed. Be careful not to pull the new yarn too tightly, or one edge of the scarf will end up tighter than the other, and arch into a curve rather than a straight rectangle.

yfsl1yo: Bring yarn to front, slip one st purlwise, yarnover

brk: With yarn at the back of work, insert the right needle tip into both a stitch and its companion yarnover knitwise. Work together as one knit stitch.

Instructions

CO 3 sts.

INCREASE SECTION

Row 1: (RS) K1, yfsl1yo, k1 tbl.

Row 2: (inc, WS) Sl1 wyf, [brk, yo, brk] into next st, p1—5 sts.

Row 3: Sl1 wyb, yfsl1yo, k1, yfsl1yo, k1 tbl.

Row 4: Sl1 wyf, brk, yfsl1yo, brk, p1.

Row 5: Sl1 wyb, yfsl1yo, brk, yfsl1yo, k1 tbl.

Row 6: (inc) Sl1 wyf, [brk, yo, brk] into next st, yfsl1yo, [brk, yo, brk] into next st, p1—9 sts.

Row 7: Sl1 wyb, yfsl1yo, k1, yfsl1yo, brk, [yfsl1yo, k1] 2 times.

Row 8: Sl1 wyf, [brk, yfsl1yo] 3 times, brk, p1.

Row 9: Sl1 wyb, [yfsl1yo, brk] 3 times, yfsl1yo, k1 tbl.

Inc row: (WS) Sl1 wyf, [brk, yo, brk] into next st, *brk, yfsl1yo; rep from * to last 2 sts, [brk, yo, brk] into next st, p1—4 sts inc'd.

Next row: (RS) Sl1 wyb, yfsl1yo, k1, *yfsl1yo, brk; rep from * to last 4 sts, [yfsl1yo, k1] 2 times.

Next row: Sl1 wyf, brk, *yfsl1yo, brk; rep from * to last st, p1.

Next row: Sl1 wyb, yfsl1yo, *brk, yfsl1yo; rep from * to last st, k1 tbl.

Rep the last 4 rows 8 more times—45 sts.

WORK-EVEN SECTION

Shift row: (WS) Sl1 wyf, cdd, yfsl1yo, *brk, yfsl1yo; rep from * to last 2 sts, [brk1, yo, brk1] into next st, p1.

Next row: (RS) Sl1 wyb, yfsl1yo, k1, *yfsl1yo, brk; rep from * to last 2 sts, yfsl1yo, k1 tbl.

Next row: Sl1 wyf, brk, *yfsl1yo, brk; rep from * to last st, p1.

Next row: Sl1 wyb, yfsl1yo, *brk, yfsl1yo; rep from * to last st, k1 tbl.

Rep the last 4 rows until scarf measures 60" (152.5 cm) or desired length from cast-on, measuring along the longest edge.

|||||||||||||||||||||||||||||||||||||||||||||||

NOTE: *If you adjust the length of your scarf, be sure you have at least 25 yd (23 m) of yarn remaining for the decrease section.*

|||||||||||||||||||||||||||||||||||||||||||||||

DECREASE SECTION

Dec row: (WS) Sl1 wyf, cdd, yfsl1yo, *brk, yfsl1yo; rep from * to last 4 sts, cdd, p1—4 sts dec'd.

Next row: (RS) Sl1 wyb, *yfsl1yo, brk; rep from * to last 2 sts, yfsl1yo, k1 tbl.

Next row: Sl1 wyf, brk, *yfsl1yo, brk; rep from * to last st, p1.

Next row: Sl1 wyb, yfsl1yo, *brk, yfsl1yo; rep from * to last st, k1 tbl.

Rep the last 4 rows 9 more times—5 sts.

Next dec row: (WS) Sl1 wyf, cdd, p1—3 sts.

Next dec row: (RS) K3tog. Fasten off.

FINISHING

Weave in ends. Block to measurements.

House Blend
CARDIGAN

The House Blend Cardigan is the cozy sweater you get into on a Saturday morning and don't take off unless you absolutely have to. It's an especially long cardigan, ending at this below-average-heighted designer's knees, and is knit from the bottom up in pieces and seamed. The yak in the yarn makes it super warm and luxurious to knit. — HANNAH BAKER

⅂⅂⅂⅂⅂⅂⅂⅂⅂⅂⅂⅂⅂⅂⅂⅂⅂⅂⅂⅂⅂⅂⅂⅂⅂⅂⅂⅂⅂⅂⅂⅂

FINISHED SIZE
About 38 (42, 46, 50, 54, 58)" (96.5 [106.5, 117, 127, 137, 147.5] cm).

Garment shown measures 42" (106.5 cm), modeled with 8" (20.5 cm) of ease.

YARN
Worsted weight (#4 medium).

Shown here: The Yarn Collective Hudson Worsted (85% Merino wool, 15% yak; 197 yd [180 m]/3½ oz [100 g]): #404 army, 8 (9, 9, 10, 11, 11) skeins.

NEEDLES
Size U.S. 8 (5 mm).

Adjust needle size if necessary to obtain the correct gauge.

NOTIONS
Stitch holders or waste yarn; removable stitch markers (rm); tapestry needle; five 27 mm/1⅛" buttons.

GAUGE
25.5 sts and 22 rows = 4" (10 cm) in 1x1 rib after blocking.

18 sts and 25.5 rows = 4" (10 cm) in Stockinette st after blocking.

NOTES
— This cardigan is knit from the bottom up, worked back and forth in pieces, and seamed.

— Use a circular needle to accommodate many stitches.

5-stitch 1-row buttonhole

Work to where you want the buttonhole to begin, bring yarn to front, sl1 purlwise, bring yarn to back.

*Sl1 purlwise, pass first slipped st over second; repeat from * 4 more times.

Place last st back on left needle, turn.

Cast on 6 sts as follows: *Insert right needle between the first and second sts on left needle, draw up a loop, and place it on the left needle; repeat from * 5 more times, turn.

Bring yarn to back, slip first st on left needle onto right needle and pass last cast-on st over it, work to end of row.

German short-rows (also see Techniques)

With yarn in front, sl1 purlwise from left needle to right needle. Pull yarn to back of work over needle until both legs of st in row below are on top of needle, creating a "double stitch" on both sides of needle. When working the double st on subsequent rows, work both legs together as a single st.

Instructions

BACK

CO 127 (141, 153, 167, 179, 193) sts.

Row 1: (WS) P2, *k1, p1; rep from * to last st, p1.

Row 2: (RS) K2, *p1, k1; rep from * to last st, k1.

Rep Rows 1 and 2 until piece measures 8" (20.5 cm) from CO, ending with a WS row.

Dec row: (RS) K1, [k2tog, k2] 5 (6, 6, 7, 7, 8) times, [k2tog, k1] 28 (30, 34, 36, 40, 42) times, [k2tog, k2] 5 (6, 6, 7, 7, 8) times, k2tog—88 (98, 106, 116, 124, 134) sts.

Work in Stockinette st until piece measures 36" (91.5 cm) from CO, ending with a WS row.

SHOULDER AND NECK SHAPING

German short-row 1: (RS) Knit to last 6 (7, 8, 9, 10, 11) sts, turn.

German short-row 2: (WS) Make double st (see Stitch Guide), purl to last 6 (7, 8, 9, 10, 11) sts, turn.

German short-row 3: Make double st, knit to 6 (7, 8, 9, 10, 11) sts before gap, turn.

German short-row 4: Make double st, purl to 6 (7, 8, 9, 10, 11) sts before gap, turn.

German short-rows 5 and 6: Rep short-rows 3 and 4.

German short-row 7: Make double st, k21 (23, 25, 26, 27, 29), BO 10 (10, 8, 10, 10, 10) sts, knit to 6 (7, 8, 9, 10, 11) sts before gap, turn. Set right shoulder sts aside on stitch holder or spare cable.

FINISH LEFT SHOULDER

German short-row 8: (WS) Make double st, purl to end, turn.

Next row: (RS) BO 9 (10, 9, 9, 9, 10) sts, knit to end, knitting double sts as 1 st; turn.

Next row: BO all sts.

FINISH RIGHT SHOULDER

Place held sts back on needle.

German short-row 8: (WS) With WS facing, join yarn to right back. Purl to 6 (7, 8, 9, 10, 11) sts before gap, turn.

German short-row 9: (RS) Make double st, knit to end, turn.

Next row: BO 9 (10, 9, 9, 9, 10) sts, purl to end, purling double sts as 1 st; turn.

Next row: BO all sts.

RIGHT FRONT (WITH BUTTONHOLES)

CO 64 (70, 78, 84, 90, 96) sts.

Row 1: (WS) P2, *k1, p1; rep from * to end.

Row 2: (RS) Sl1, *p1, k1; rep from * to last st, k1.

Rep Rows 1 and 2 until piece measures 8" (20.5 cm) from CO, ending with a WS row.

Buttonhole row/dec row: (RS) Sl1, work 8 sts in rib patt as established, work 5-stitch 1-row buttonhole (see Stitch Guide), work 9 sts in rib patt, [k2tog, k2] 3 (3, 4, 4, 4, 4) times, [k2tog, k1] 5 (7, 7, 9, 11, 13) times, [k2tog, k2] 3 (3, 4, 4, 4, 4) times, k2tog —52 (56, 62, 66, 70, 74) sts rem.

Next row: (WS) P29 (33, 39, 43, 47, 51), work in rib patt to end.

Next row: (RS) Sl1, work 22 sts in rib patt, knit to end.

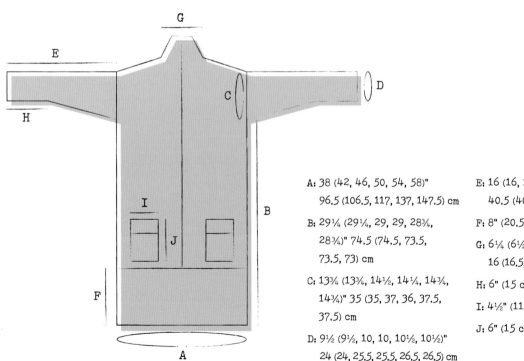

A: 38 (42, 46, 50, 54, 58)"
96.5 (106.5, 117, 137, 147.5) cm

B: 29¼ (29¼, 29, 29, 28¾, 28¾)" 74.5 (74.5, 73.5, 73.5, 73) cm

C: 13¾ (13¾, 14½, 14¼, 14¾, 14¾)" 35 (35, 37, 36, 37.5, 37.5) cm

D: 9½ (9½, 10, 10, 10½, 10½)" 24 (24, 25.5, 25.5, 26.5, 26.5) cm

E: 16 (16, 16½, 16½, 17, 17)" 40.5 (40.5, 42, 42, 43, 43) cm

F: 8" (20.5 cm)

G: 6¼ (6½, 5¾, 6¼, 6¼, 6½)" 16 (16.5, 14.5, 16, 16, 16.5) cm

H: 6" (15 cm)

I: 4½" (11.5 cm)

J: 6" (15 cm)

Rep last 2 rows for 4¼" (11 cm) (until piece measures 12¼" [31 cm]), ending with a WS row.

Buttonhole row: (RS) Sl1, work 8 sts in rib patt, work 5-stitch 1-row buttonhole, work 9 sts in rib patt, knit to end.

Next row: (WS) P29 (33, 39, 43, 47, 51), work in rib patt to end.

Next row: (RS) Sl1, work 22 sts in rib patt, knit to end.

Next row: (WS) P29 (33, 39, 43, 47, 51), work in rib patt to end.

Work in established patt, working buttonhole row every 4¼" (11 cm) 3 more times—5 buttonholes worked.

Piece measures about 25" (63.5 cm) from CO.

Work even in established patt until piece measures 29¼ (29¼, 29, 29, 28¾, 28¾)" (74.5 [74.5, 73.5, 73.5, 73, 73] cm) from CO; mark this row with rm, then continue in patt until piece measures 36" (91.5 cm) from CO, ending with a WS row.

BEGIN SHOULDER SHAPING

German short-row 1: (RS) Work in patt to last 6 (7, 8, 9, 10, 11) sts, turn.

German short-row 2: (WS) Make double st (see Stitch Guide), work in patt to end.

German short-row 3: Work in patt to 6 (7, 8, 9, 10, 11) sts before gap, turn.

German short-row 4: Rep German short-row 2.

German short-rows 5–8: Rep German short-rows 3 and 4.

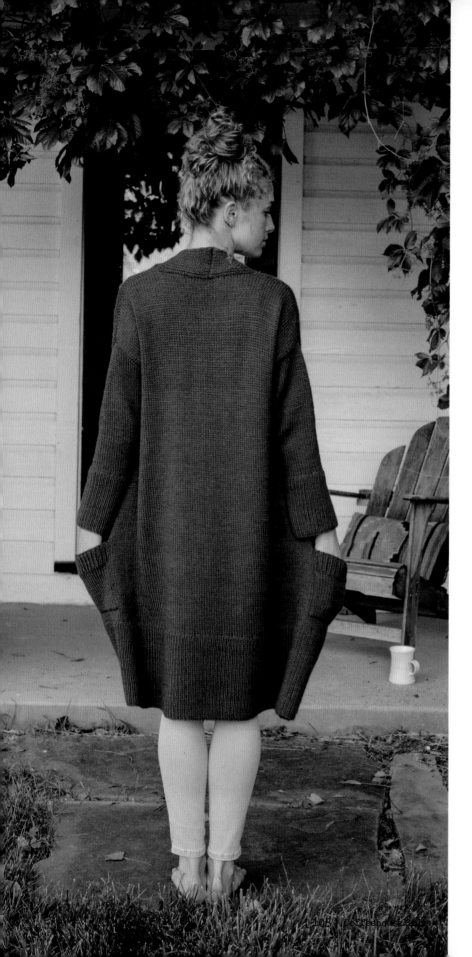

German short-row 9: Work in patt to 6 (6, 8, 8, 8, 8) sts before gap, turn.

German short-row 10: Rep German short-row 2.

Next row: (RS) Work 22 sts in patt, then knit to end, knitting double sts as 1 st.

Next row: (WS) BO 30 (34, 40, 44, 48, 52) sts, work in rib patt to end.

Work in rib patt for 3⅛ (3¼, 2⅞, 3⅛, 3⅛, 3¼)" (8 [8.5, 7.5, 8, 8, 8.5] cm). Put sts on holder.

LEFT FRONT (NO BUTTONHOLES)

CO 64 (70, 78, 84, 90, 96) sts.

Row 1: (WS) Sl1, k1, *p1, k1; rep from * to last 2 sts, p2.

Row 2: (RS) K2, *p1, k1; rep from * to end.

Rep Rows 1 and 2 until piece measures 8" (20.5 cm) from CO, ending with a WS row.

Dec row: (RS) K1, [k2tog, k2] 3 (3, 4, 4, 4, 4) times, [k2tog, k1] 5 (7, 7, 9, 11, 13) times, [k2tog, k2] 3 (3, 4, 4, 4, 4) times, k2tog, work in rib patt to end—52 (56, 62, 66, 70, 74) sts.

Next row: (WS) Sl1, work in rib patt for 21 sts, purl to end.

Next row: (RS) Knit to last 22 sts, work in rib patt to end.

Rep last 2 rows until piece measures 29¼ (29¼, 29, 29, 28¾, 28¾)" (74.5 [74.5, 73.5, 73.5, 73, 73] cm) from CO;

mark this row with rm, then continue in patt until piece measures 36" (91.5 cm) from CO, ending with a RS row.

BEGIN SHOULDER SHAPING

German short-row 1: (WS) Work in patt to 6 (7, 8, 9, 10, 11) sts before end of row, turn.

German short-row 2: (RS) Make double st (see Stitch Guide), work in patt to end.

German short-row 3: Work in patt to 6 (7, 8, 9, 10, 11) sts before gap, turn.

German short-row 4: Rep German short-row 1.

German short-rows 5–8: Rep German short-rows 3 and 4.

German short-row 9: Work in patt to 6 (6, 8, 8, 8, 8) sts before gap, turn.

German short-row 10: Rep German short-row 2.

Next row: (WS) Work in rib patt for 22 sts, then purl to end, purling double sts as 1 st.

Next row: (RS) BO 30 (34, 40, 44, 48, 52) sts, work in rib patt to end.

Work in rib patt for 3⅛ (3¼, 2⅞, 3⅛, 3⅛, 3¼)" (8 [8.5, 7.5, 8, 8, 8.5] cm). Put sts on holder.

SLEEVES (MAKE 2)

CO 62 (62, 66, 66, 70, 70) sts.

Row 1: (WS) *P1, k1; rep from * to end.

Row 2: (RS) *K1, p1; rep from * to end.

Rep these 2 rows for 6" (15 cm), ending with a WS row.

Dec row: (RS) K1, [k2tog, k2] 4 (4, 3, 3, 2, 2) times, [k2tog, k1] 9 (9, 13, 13, 17, 17) times, [k2tog, k2] 4 (4, 3, 3, 2, 2) times, k2tog—44 (44, 46, 46, 48, 48) sts.

Next row: (WS) Purl to end.

Work even in St st for 5 (5, 5, 5, 7, 7) rows.

Inc row: (RS) K1, M1R, knit to last st, M1L, k1—2 sts inc'd.

Next row: (WS) Purl to end.

Work in St st, repeating Inc row every 6 (6, 6, 6, 7, 7) rows 8 more times —62 (62, 64, 64, 66, 66) sts.

Work even until sleeve measures 16 (16, 16½, 16½, 17, 17)" from CO.

BO all sts.

POCKETS

CO 31 sts.

Row 1: (WS) *K1, p1; rep from * to last st, k1.

Row 2: (RS) *P1, k1; rep from * to last st, p1.

Cont in rib patt for 2" (5 cm), ending with a WS row.

Dec row: (RS) *K1, k2tog; rep from * to last st, k—21 sts.

Work in St st until piece measures 6" (15 cm) from CO.

BO all sts.

FINISHING

Block pieces to finished measurements.

Seam shoulders together using mattress stitch (see Techniques).

Seam fronts to back from bottom up using mattress stitch, stopping at rm. Remove markers.

Seam neck ribbing to back neck.

Join neck ribbing sts using three-needle bind-off (see Techniques).

Seam sleeve caps to armhole using mattress stitch.

Seam sleeves.

Sew pockets to fronts of cardigan. The bottom of each pocket should sit 1" (2.5 cm) above the top of the ribbed hem, and the edge of each pocket should sit 1" (2.5 cm) in from the ribbed edging of the cardigan front.

Sew buttons onto left front opposite each buttonhole, about 1" (2.5 cm) in from edge. Weave in ends.

Knitting has given me new
confidence. Over the past
few years, knitting has
been an incredible asset to
socialization.

THE WORLD IS OUR COFFEEHOUSE: KNITTING FOR INTROVERTS

by Melody Hoffmann

AS A DEEPLY INTROVERTED person, I find it really hard to express myself sometimes, whether it be through words or gestures. In that regard, knitting is a wonderful medium to express emotions, feelings, sensations that I don't always have words for.

I remember many years ago, when I was living in China, I stumbled across a group of ladies sitting on tiny stools outside of a shop. They were all chatting vividly and knitting toddler garments on the tiniest double-pointed needles I had ever seen. I had just learned how to knit and didn't know much about knitting, but was completely mesmerized.

At the time, I thought my knitting was not good enough—and let's be honest, my shyness was probably in the way, too—to engage in a conversation with them about knitting, much less to look over their shoulders to have a proper look at their techniques. But my present-day self would not hesitate to have a seat, take my knitting out, and ask them to teach me some of their amazing skills.

What has changed is that knitting has given me new confidence. Over the past few years, knitting has been an incredible asset to socialization, which helped me to come out of my shell a little bit and foster connections with fellow knitters.

A few years ago I attended a knitting workshop here in Riga, Latvia, on how to knit traditional Latvian mittens. I do not speak Latvian at all, so I wasn't able to grasp a thing about the historical part of the workshop, but I was able to follow the practical part a little bit better, though it was very challenging, I must say—not language-wise, but because the techniques were completely new to me, and apparently it takes quite a bit of time for my brain to process all the information . . .

We learned what I think is called the Bulgarian cast-on, which is similar to the long-tail cast-on, though much more complicated! Even though the lecture part of the course wasn't accessible to me, I was able, through knitting, to be introduced to a part of a culture that was foreign to me.

From admiring from afar a group of ladies knitting, to attending a workshop in a different language, to interacting with fellow knitters through social media, to actually meeting knitters that I first met online, my life as a knitter has evolved. Before sharing my passion and work on Instagram, I had no clue, first of all, that there were so many knitters in the world! And second of all, that so many different cultures were sharing the same interest in this fiber craft!

Social media is its own sort of coffeehouse, isn't it? From my tiny bedroom at my parents', where I first started knitting, I was now able to connect with knitters from everywhere in the world and interact with people from completely different cultures who nevertheless shared the exact same interest as me. Stitches, cables, colorwork, increases, charts . . . they might have different names in each language, but they all mean the same to knitters. —

Extra Whip SOCKS

I like my coffee blonde and sweet with extra whipped topping. The gentle cables of these socks are spaced generously, to allow for some down time to chat while knitting, but still evoke the twisty whipped-cream topping of your favorite espresso drink. These socks are the perfect fall and winter accessory, giving a playful feel to cold-weather dressing. — **KATHERINE ROLLINS**

ʈʌʈʌʈʌʈʌʈʌʈʌʈʌʈʌʈʌʈʌʈʌʈʌʈʌ

FINISHED SIZE
About 7 (8, 9)" (18 [20.5, 23] cm) foot circumference.

Project shown measures 7" (18 cm).

YARN
Fingering weight (#1 superfine).

Shown here: Lorna's Laces Shepherd Sock (80% superwash Merino wool, 20% nylon; 435 yd [398 m]/3½ oz [100 g]): natural, 1 skein.

NEEDLES
Size U.S. 1–2½ (2.25–3 mm) double-pointed (dpn) or 32" (80 cm) circular (cir) for magic loop method.

Adjust needle size if necessary to obtain the correct gauge.

NOTIONS
Stitch markers (m); cable needle (cn); stitch holder or spare needle; tapestry needle.

GAUGE
36 sts and 52 rnds = 4" (10 cm) in Stockinette st after blocking.

NOTE
— On the toe, knit the knit sts and purl the purl sts to maintain the Rib Pattern between the first and last two stitches on the top of the sock.

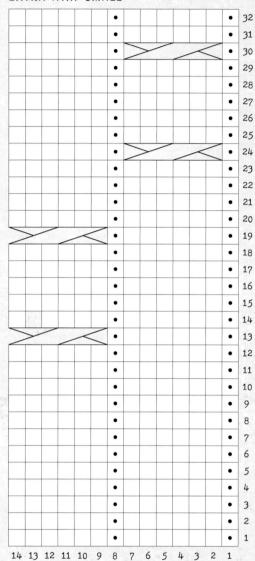

Rib pattern:

Size 7" (18 cm) only

*P1, k6; rep from * to end.

Size 8" (20.5 cm) only

P1, k6, *p2, k6; rep
from * to last st, p1.

Size 9" (23 cm) only

P1, k6, *p3, k6; rep from
* to last 2 sts, p2.

3/3 RC

On RS: Slip 4 sts to cn
and hold in back, k3,
slip 1 st from cn to left
needle and move cn to
front, k1, k3 from cn.

Instructions

CUFF

CO 56 (64, 72) sts loosely.

Pm and join for working in the
round, being careful not to twist.

Work 4 rnds of Rib pattern
(see Stitch Guide).

LEG

Work Rows 1–32 of Extra Whip
Chart Small (Medium, Large). Chart
is repeated 4 times around leg.

After completing chart, work
4 rnds of Rib pattern.

EXTRA WHIP SMALL

☐ knit

• purl

⤬ 3/3RC

SET UP FOR HEEL FLAP

Work 28 (32, 36) sts in Rib pattern, then set these instep sts aside on nonworking needle or stitch holder.

HEEL FLAP

The heel flap will be worked back and forth over the next 28 (32, 36) sts.

Row 1: (RS) *Sl1, k1; rep from * to end, turn.

Row 2: (WS) Sl1, purl to end.

Rep these 2 rows 15 (17, 19) more times.

TURN HEEL

Row 1: Sl1, k15 (17, 19), ssk, k1, turn.

Row 2: Sl1, p5, p2tog, p1, turn.

Row 3: Sl1, knit to 1 st before the gap, ssk (closing the gap), k1, turn.

Row 4: Sl1, purl to 1 st before the gap, p2tog (closing the gap), p1, turn.

Rep Rows 3 and 4 until all heel sts have been worked, ending with a WS row. Omit the final k1 or p1 on the last 2 rows.

Next row: Knit to end—16 (18, 20) heel sts.

GUSSET

Pick up and knit 16 (18, 20) sts along edge of heel flap, pm, work Row 1 of Extra Whip Chart Small (Medium, Large) across instep sts, pm, pick up and knit 16 (18, 20) sts along other edge of heel flap, k8 (9, 10) and pm for beg of rnd—76 (86, 96) sts.

Rnd 1: Knit to m, work Extra Whip Chart to m, knit to end.

Rnd 2: Knit to 3 sts before m, k2tog, k1, work Extra Whip Chart to m, k1, ssk, knit to end.

Rep Rnds 1 and 2 until 56 (64, 72) sts rem.

Knit to first m (at beg of instep); this is the new beg of rnd. Remove all other markers as you work the next rnd.

FOOT

Next rnd: Work Extra Whip Chart as established across instep, knit to end.

Rep this rnd until foot is 2" (5 cm) shorter than desired total foot length. Rep chart as necessary, ending at least 2 rows beyond a cable row.

TOE

Rnd 1: Work Rib pattern over 28 (32, 36) sts, pm, knit to end.

Rnd 2: K1, ssk, work Rib pattern as established to 3 sts before m, k2tog, k2, ssk, knit to last 3 sts, k2tog, k1.

Rnd 3: Work sts as they appear (knit the knit sts and purl the purl sts).

Rnd 4: Rep Rnd 2.

Rep Rnds 3 and 4 until 28 (32, 36) sts rem.

Rep Rnd 2 until 16 sts rem.

Graft rem sts together using Kitchener stitch (see Techniques).

FINISHING

Weave in ends. Block to finished measurements.

EXTRA WHIP MEDIUM

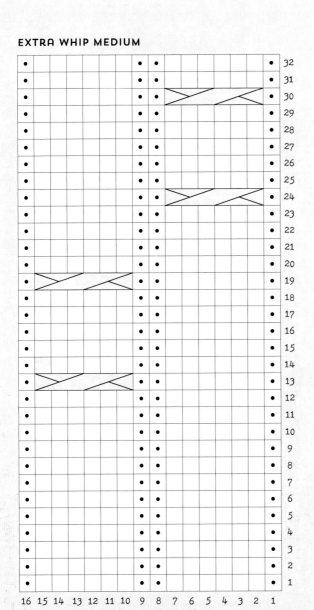

EXTRA WHIP LARGE

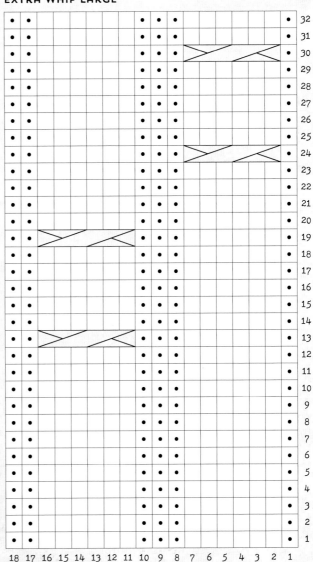

	knit
•	purl

 3/3RC

CAFÉ *Cowl*

Originating in the British Isles, the houndstooth pattern may historically be more often paired with tea than coffee, but will be a great companion to any cozy drink of your choice. It looks harder than it is! The two-stitch, four-row slipped-stitch colorwork houndstooth pattern uses only one color per row, creating a modern, easy cowl. — **JENNIFER DASSAU**

FINISHED SIZE
About 10" (25.5 cm) tall and 26" (66 cm) circumference.

YARN
Worsted weight (#4 medium).

Shown here: Blue Sky Fibers Woolstok Worsted (100% fine highland wool; 123 yd [112 m]/1¾ oz [50 g]): 1314 deep velvet (MC), 1 skein; 1312 drift wood (CC), 1 skein.

NEEDLES
Size U.S. 8 (5 mm): 24" (60 cm) circular (cir).

Adjust needle size if necessary to obtain the correct gauge.

NOTIONS
Stitch marker (m); tapestry needle.

GAUGE
16 sts and 34 rnds = 4" (10 cm) in houndstooth patt, unblocked.

NOTES
— This cowl is cast on at the bottom edge, joined in the round, and worked in a houndstooth slipped-stitch pattern with garter-stitch edges.

— Cowl can be worn with top or bottom edge up, according to preference.

Instructions

Using MC and long-tail cast-on, CO 108 sts; pm and join for working in the round, being careful not to twist.

GARTER EDGE (MC)

Rnd 1: Knit to end.

Rnd 2: Purl to end.

Rep Rnds 1 and 2 five more times.

HOUNDSTOOTH PATTERN

Rnd 1: With CC, *sl1 wyb, k1; rep from * to end.

Rnd 2: Purl.

Rnd 3: With MC, *k1, sl1 wyb; rep from * to end.

Rnd 4: Purl.

Rep Rnds 1–4 fourteen more times. Cowl measures about 8½" (21.5 cm) from CO edge. Cut MC yarn.

GARTER EDGE (CC)

Rnd 1: Knit to end.

Rnd 2: Purl to end.

Rep Rnds 1 and 2 five more times.

BO all sts purlwise.

FINISHING

Weave in ends; leaving the cowl unblocked will preserve the integrity and density of the houndstooth pattern and the garter stitch. If you must, steam-block lightly and lay flat to dry, without stretching.

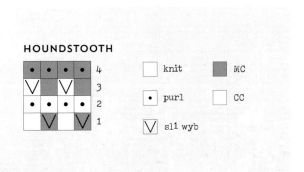

HOUNDSTOOTH

	knit		MC
•	purl		CC
V	sl1 wyb		

FROTHY

The Frothy Pullover was designed to be a simple knit, but also to be savored like a good cup of coffee—it's light and airy, like a head of foam. It features a twisted purl-stitch pattern worked in a fingering-weight Merino wool. The purl clusters in this easy-to-remember stitch pattern create an interesting texture and lacy eyelet effect without requiring any yarnovers. — **CATRINA FROST**

FINISHED SIZE

About 36 (40, 44, 48, 52, 56)" (91.5 [101.5, 112, 122, 132, 142] cm) bust circumference.

Garment shown measures 36" (91.5 cm), modeled with 2" (5 cm) of ease.

YARN

Fingering weight (#1 superfine).

Shown here: Hedgehog Fibres Sock (90% superwash Merino wool, 10% nylon; 437 yd [400 m]/3½ oz [100 g]): pine, 3 (4, 5, 5, 6, 6) skeins.

NEEDLES

Size U.S. 3 (3.25 mm): 32" (80 cm) circular (cir); set of double-pointed (dpn) or preferred method for small-circumference knitting.

Size U.S. 4 (3.5 mm): 32" (80 cm) cir.

Adjust needle size if necessary to obtain the correct gauge.

NOTIONS

Stitch markers (m); waste yarn or stitch holders; tapestry needle.

GAUGE

28 sts and 26 rnds = 4" (10 cm) in Twisted Purl st patt on larger needle after blocking.

32 sts and 34 rnds = 4" (10 cm) in Stockinette st on smaller needle after blocking.

NOTES

— Be sure to knit your gauge swatch in the round for accurate gauge.

— When working flat, treat odd-numbered Twisted Purl Stitch rounds as right-side rows.

— Selvedge stitches in the yoke are not included in final measurements.

Twisted Purl Stitch (4 sts)

Rnd 1: (RS) *K2, p2tog and without removing sts from the left needle, purl first st again, then slip both sts off; rep from * to end.

Rnd 2: If working in the round, knit to end; if working flat, purl to end.

Rnd 3: *P2tog and without removing sts from the left needle, purl first st again, then slip both sts off; k2, rep from * to end.

Rnd 4: If working in the round, knit to end; if working flat, purl to end.

Instructions

BODY

With smaller 32" (80 cm) cir needle, CO 252 (280, 308, 336, 364, 392) sts. Pm and join for working in the round, being careful not to twist.

Rnd 1: *K2, p2; rep from * to end.

Rep Rnd 1 nine more times.

Switch to larger needle and knit 1 rnd.

Work in Twisted Purl Stitch patt (see Stitch Guide) until piece measures 15 (15, 16, 16, 17, 17)" (38 [38, 40.5, 40.5, 43, 43] cm) from cast-on edge.

DIVIDE FOR FRONT AND BACK

Work 126 (140, 154, 168, 182, 196) sts in patt, place rem 126 (140, 154, 168, 182, 196) sts on holder for back.

Turn work and begin working back and forth in rows.

||||||||||||||||||||||||||||||||||||||||||||||||||||

> **NOTE:** *Some sizes will now have a stitch count that isn't evenly divisible by four (the Twisted Purl Stitch repeat); for these sizes, work the last two sts in patt as established.*

||||||||||||||||||||||||||||||||||||||||||||||||||||

FRONT

On the next 2 rows, you'll add 1 selvedge stitch to each edge. These stitches should be worked in garter stitch (knit on RS and WS) on all following rows.

Next row: (WS) CO 1 st (selvedge), knit the selvedge st, work in patt to end.

Next row: (RS) CO 1 st (selvedge), knit the selvedge st, work in patt to last st, k1—128 (142, 156, 170, 184, 198) sts.

Continue working in Twisted Purl Stitch patt, maintaining garter-stitch selvedge sts, until armhole measures 7 (7½, 8, 8½, 9, 9½)" (18 [19, 20.5, 21.5, 23, 24] cm), ending with a WS row.

Next row: (RS) Work 32 (39, 43, 50, 53, 60) sts in patt, BO 64 (64, 70, 70, 78, 78) neck sts, work in patt to end.

Place shoulder sts on stitch holders and break yarn, leaving a 16" (40 cm) tail for seaming.

BACK

Return 126 (140, 154, 168, 182, 196) held sts to larger 32" (80 cm) cir needle and rejoin yarn.

Work 1 RS row in patt.

Next row: (WS) CO 1 st (selvedge), knit the selvedge st, work in patt to end.

Next row: (RS) CO 1 st (selvedge), knit the selvedge st, work in patt to end —128 (142, 156, 170, 184, 198) sts.

Continue working in Twisted Purl Stitch patt, maintaining garter-stitch selvedge sts, until armhole measures 7 (7½, 8, 8½, 9, 9½)" (18 [19, 20.5, 21.5, 23, 24] cm), ending with a WS row.

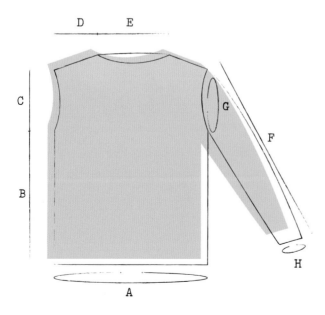

A: 36 (40, 44, 48, 52, 56)"
91.5 (101.5, 112, 122, 132, 142) cm

B: 15 (15, 16, 16, 17, 17)"
38 (38, 40.5, 40.5, 43, 43) cm

C: 7 (7½, 8, 8½, 9, 9½)"
18 (19, 20.5, 21.5, 24) cm

D: 4½ (5½, 6, 7, 7½, 8½)"
11.5 (14, 15, 18, 19, 21.5) cm

E: 9¼ (9¼, 10, 10, 11¼, 11¼)"
23.5 (23.5, 25.5, 25.5, 26, 26) cm

F: 19 (19, 19, 20, 20, 20)"
48.5 (48.5, 48.5, 51, 51, 51) cm

G: 12 (12¾, 14¼, 14¾, 15¾, 16¾)"
30.5 (32, 36, 37.5, 40, 42.5) cm

H: 7½ (7½, 9, 9½, 10½, 11½)"
19 (19, 23, 24, 26.5, 29) cm

Next row: (RS) Work 32 (39, 43, 50, 53, 60) sts in patt, BO 64 (64, 70, 70, 78, 78) neck sts, work in patt to end.

JOIN SHOULDERS

Return held shoulder sts to dpn. Hold front and back pieces with RS together (WS facing out) and join shoulder sts using three-needle bind-off (see Techniques).

SLEEVES

With RS facing and smaller dpn or small-circumference needle, starting at underarm, pick up and knit 96 (102, 114, 118, 126, 134) sts evenly around the armhole edge. Pm and join for working in the round.

Knit 16 rnds in St st.

Dec rnd: K1, k2tog, knit to last 3 sts, ssk, k1—2 sts dec'd.

Rep Dec rnd every fourth rnd 17 (20, 20, 20, 20, 20) more times —60 (60, 72, 76, 84, 92) sts.

Work even in St st until sleeve measures 17 (17, 17, 18, 18, 18)" (43 [43, 43, 45.5, 45.5, 45.5] cm).

Next rnd: *K2, p2; rep from * to end.

Rep last rnd 14 more times.

BO all sts loosely in patt.

FINISHING

Weave in ends and block to finished measurements.

Steamed MITTENS

These lovely mittens are the perfect coffeeshop knit. The simple knit and purl patterning on the main part of the mitten is easily memorized and gives the mittens great texture. The patterning just above the cuff starts with a couple of rounds of seed stitch. The purl dots then spread out and are worked farther apart as they get closer to the top of the mitten, like steam evaporating into the air. — EMILY KINTIGH

ιιιιιιιιιιιιιιιιιιιιιιιιιιιιιιιιιιιιιιιιιι

FINISHED SIZE

About 6 (6¾, 7¼, 8)" (15 [17, 18.5, 20.5] cm) hand circumference.

Project shown measures 7¼" (18.5 cm).

YARN

Worsted weight (#4 medium).

Shown here: Berroco Ultra Alpaca (50% superfine alpaca, 50% Peruvian wool; 215 yd [197 m]/3½ oz [100 g]): 62189 barley, 1 skein.

NEEDLES

Size U.S. 4 (3.5 mm): double-pointed (dpn) or long circular (cir) for magic loop method (see Techniques).

Size U.S. 6 (4 mm): dpn or long cir for magic loop method.

Adjust needle size if necessary to obtain the correct gauge.

NOTIONS

Stitch markers (m); waste yarn or stitch holder; tapestry needle.

GAUGE

24 sts and 34 rnds = 4" (10 cm) in Steamed 2 Chart patt on larger needle after blocking.

NOTE

— Mittens are worked in the round from the cuff up. Thumb stitches are placed on a holder and worked last, also in the round.

2x2 ribbing

All rnds: *K2, p2;
rep from * to end.

Instructions

CUFF

With smaller needle, CO 36 (40, 44, 48) sts. Pm and join for working in the round, being careful not to twist. Work in 2x2 ribbing (see Stitch guide) for 2¾ (3, 3¼, 3½)" (7 [7.5, 8.5, 9] cm) or desired cuff length.

THUMB GUSSET

Switch to larger needle.

Rnd 1: *K1, p1; rep from * to end.

Rnd 2: M1L, pm, *p1, k1; rep from * to end—37 (41, 45, 49) sts.

Rnd 3: K1, sl m, *k1, p1; rep from * to end.

Rnd 4: M1L, knit to m, M1R, sl m, *p1, k3; rep from * to end—39 (43, 47, 51) sts.

Rnd 5: Knit to end.

Rnd 6: M1L, knit to m, M1R, sl m, *k2, p1, k1; rep from * to end—41 (45, 49, 53) sts.

Rnd 7: Knit to end.

Rep Rnds 4–7 two (three, three, four) more times, then Rnds 4 and 5 one (zero, one, zero) more time(s)—51 (57, 63, 69) sts.

MAIN MITTEN

Rnd 1: Slip first 15 (17, 19, 21) sts onto waste yarn or stitch holder, remove m, knit to end—36 (40, 44, 48) sts.

Continue working in the round and begin working Steamed 2 Chart as specified below. Chart is repeated 9 (10, 11, 12) times around hand.

6" (15 cm) size only

Work chart Rnds 4–6, then Rnds 1–6.

6¾" (17 cm) size only

Work chart Rnds 1–6 twice.

7¼" (18.5 cm) size only

Work chart Rnds 4–6, then Rnds 1–6 twice.

8" (20.5 cm) size only

Work chart Rnds 1–6 three times.

All sizes

Begin working Steamed 3 Chart. Work Rnds 1–8, then Rnds 1–4. Knit all rnds until mitten measures 6 (6¼, 6½, 6¾)" (15 [16, 16.5, 17] cm) from top of cuff.

FINGERTIP

6" (15 cm) size only

*K7, k2tog; rep from * to end—32 sts. Work Decreases (below) beginning with Rnd 2.

6¾" (17 cm) size only

Work Decreases (below) beginning with Rnd 1.

7¼" (18.5 cm) size only

*K9, k2tog; rep from * to end—40 sts. Knit 1 rnd even, then work Decreases (below) beginning with Rnd 1.

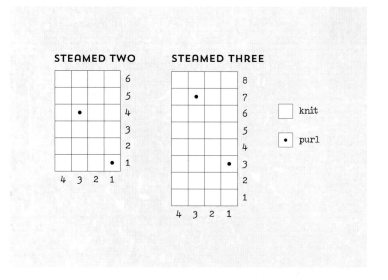

STEAMED TWO   STEAMED THREE

☐ knit

• purl

8" (20.5 cm) size only

*K4, k2tog; rep from * to end—40 sts.
Knit 1 rnd even, then work Decreases
(below) beginning with Rnd 1.

DECREASES

Rnd 1: *K3, k2tog; rep from
* to end—32 sts.

Rnd 2: Knit to end.

Rnd 3: *K2, k2tog; rep from
* to end—24 sts.

Rnd 4: Knit to end.

Rnd 5: *K1, k2tog; rep from
* to end—16 sts.

Rnd 6: Knit to end.

Rnd 7: K2tog to end—8 sts.

Cut yarn and pull through remaining sts.

THUMB

Place held sts back on larger needle. Pm and rejoin yarn to work in the round.

Rnd 1: K2tog, knit to end —14 (16, 18, 20) sts.

Knit even until thumb measures 1¾ (2¼, 2½, 2¾)" (4.5 [5.5, 6.5, 7] cm) or desired length.

7¼" (18.5 cm) size only

*K1, k2tog; rep from * to end—12 sts.

8" (20.5 cm) size only

*K3, k2tog; rep from * to end—16 sts.

All sizes

K2tog to end—7 (8, 6, 8) sts.

Cut yarn and pull through rem sts.

FINISHING

Weave in ends, making sure to close up the hole where the thumb meets the hand. Wash and lay flat to dry.

Yarn Resources

Berroco
berroco.com

Blue Sky Fibers
blueskyfibers.com

Brooklyn Tweed
brooklyntweed.com

Bumblebirch
bumblebirch.com

Fibra Natura
universalyarn.com

Hazel Knits
hazelknits.com

Hedgehog Fibres
shop.hedgehogfibres.com

Lorna's Laces
lornaslaces.net

Malabrigo
malabrigoyarn.com

Native Yarns
nativeyarns.co.uk

Purl Soho
purlsoho.com

Quince & Co.
quinceandco.com

Salt River Mills
nasurico.com

SweetGeorgia Yarns
sweetgeorgiayarns.com

Skein
skeinyarn.com

The Yarn Collective
theyarncollective.com

Universal Yarn
universalyarn.com

Western Sky Knits
wsknits.com

Woolfolk
woolfolkyarn.com

YOTH
yothyarns.com

ABBREVIATIONS

The following are the most common abbreviations that appear in this book. For other terms, be sure to check individual pattern stitch guides. For more advanced techniques or terms you don't know, please visit the Interweave online glossary: **interweave.com/ interweave-knitting-glossary/**

beg(s) begin(s); beginning

BO bind off

CC contrasting color

cdd Slip 2 stitches knitwise, knit 1, pass slipped stitches over

cir circular needle

cm centimeter(s)

cn cable needle

CO cast on

cont continue(s); continuing

dec(s) decrease(s); decreasing

dpn double-pointed needles

foll follow(s); following

g gram(s)

inc(s) increase(s); increasing

k knit

k*tog knit * stitches together

k1f&b knit into the front and back of same stitch

kwise knitwise, as if to knit

lli left lifted increase

LC left cable

m marker(s)

MC main color

mm millimeter(s)

M1 make one (increase)

M1L make one left leaning

M1P make one purlwise

M1R make one right leaning

p purl

p*tog purl * stitches together

p1f&b purl into front and back of same stitch

patt(s) pattern(s)

pm place marker

psso pass slipped stitch over

pwise purlwise, as if to purl

rem remain(s); remaining

rep repeat(s); repeating

rev St st reverse Stockinette stitch

rli right lifted increase

RC right cable

rm removable marker

rnd(s) round(s)

RS right side

skp slip a stitch, knit the next stitch, pass the slipped stitch over

sl slip (purlwise unless otherwise indicated)

ssk slip 2 stitches knitwise, one at a time, from the left needle to right needle, insert left needle tip through both front loops and knit together from this position

st(s) stitch(es)

St st stockinette stitch

tbl through back loop

tog together

w&t wrap the next stitches and turn work

WS wrong side

wyb with yarn in back

wyf with yarn in front

yd yard(s)

yfsl1yo bring yarn to front, slip 1 stitche purlwise, yarnover

yo yarnover

* repeat starting point

** repeat all instructions between asterisks

( ) alternate measurements and/or instructions

[ ] work instructions as a group a specified number of times

TECHNIQUES

Bind-offs

THREE-NEEDLE BIND-OFF

Place the stitches to be joined onto two separate needles and hold the needles parallel so that the right sides of knitting face together. Insert a third needle into the first stitch on each of two needles **(FIG. 1)** and knit them together as one stitch **(FIG. 2)**, *knit the next stitch on each needle the same way, then use the left needle tip to lift the first stitch over the second and off the needle **(FIG. 3)**. Repeat from * until no stitches remain on first two needles. Cut yarn and pull tail through last stitch to secure.

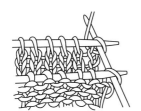

Fig. 1

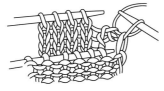

Fig. 2

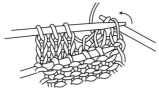

Fig. 3

I-CORD BIND-OFF

With right side facing, cast on number of stitches needed for I-cord (as directed in pattern) onto left needle **(FIG. 1)**. *Knit to last I-cord stitch (e.g., if working a three-stitch I-cord as shown, knit two), knit two together through the back loops **(FIG. 2)**, and transfer all stitches from right needle to left needle **(FIG 3)**. Repeat from * until required number of stitches have been bound off.

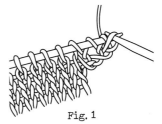

Fig. 1

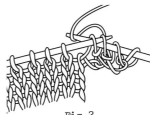

Fig. 2

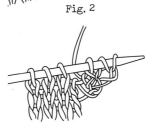

Fig. 3

Cast-ons

BACKWARD-LOOP CAST-ON

*Loop working yarn as shown and place
it on needle backward (with right leg of
loop in back of needle). Repeat from *.

KNITTED CAST-ON

Place slipknot on left needle if there
are no established stitches. *With right
needle, knit into first stitch (or slipknot)
on left needle (**FIG. 1**) and place new stitch
onto left needle (**FIG. 2**). Repeat from *,
always knitting into last stitch made.

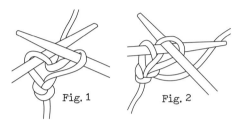

Fig. 1   Fig. 2

LONG-TAIL CAST-ON

Leaving a long tail (about 1–2" [2.5–5 cm] for each stitch to be cast on), make a slipknot and place
on right needle. Place thumb and index finger of left hand between yarn ends so that working yarn is
around index finger and tail end is around thumb. Secure ends with your other fingers and hold palm
upwards, making a V of yarn (**FIG. 1**). Bring needle up through loop on thumb (**FIG. 2**), grab first strand
around index finger with needle, and go back down through loop on thumb (**FIG. 3**). Drop loop off
thumb and, placing thumb back in V configuration, tighten resulting stitch on needle (**FIG. 4**).

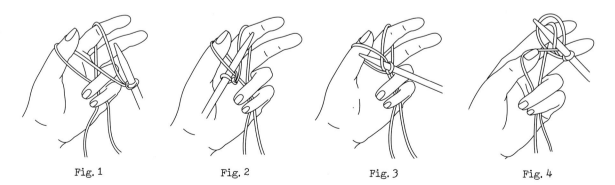

Fig. 1   Fig. 2   Fig. 3   Fig. 4

KITCHENER STITCH

Arrange stitches on two needles so that there is an equal number of stitches on each needle. Hold the needles parallel to each other with wrong sides of the knitting together. Allowing about ½" (1.3 cm) per stitch to be grafted, thread matching yarn on a tapestry needle. Work from right to left as follows:

Step 1. Bring tapestry needle through the first stitch on the front needle as if to purl and leave the stitch on the needle **(FIG. 1)**.

Step 2. Bring tapestry needle through the first stitch on the back needle as if to knit and leave that stitch on the needle **(FIG. 2)**.

Step 3. Bring tapestry needle through the first front stitch as if to knit and slip this stitch off the needle. Then bring tapestry needle

through the next front stitch as if to purl and leave this stitch on the needle **(FIG. 3)**.

Step 4. Bring tapestry needle through the first back stitch as if to purl and slip this stitch off the needle. Then bring tapestry needle through the next back stitch as if to knit and leave this stitch on the needle **(FIG. 4)**.

Repeat Steps 3 and 4 until one stitch remains on each needle, adjusting the tension to match the rest of the knitting as you go. To finish, bring tapestry needle through the front stitch as if to knit and slip this stitch off the needle. Then bring tapestry needle through the back stitch as if to purl and slip this stitch off the needle.

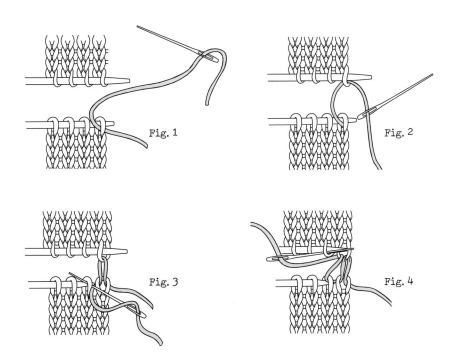

Fig. 1

Fig. 2

Fig. 3

Fig. 4

MATTRESS STITCH: VERTICAL TO VERTICAL SEAM

With RS of knitting facing, use threaded needle to pick up one bar between first two stitches on one piece, then corresponding bar plus the bar above it on other piece. *Pick up next two bars on first piece, then next two bars on other. Repeat from * to end of seam, finishing by picking up last bar (or pair of bars) at the top of first piece **(FIG. 1)**.

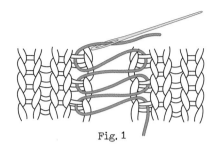

Fig. 1

MATTRESS STITCH: VERTICAL TO HORIZONTAL SEAM

This method combines the mattress stitch method of picking up the bars between stitches on the vertical edge and working under stitches along the horizontal seam **(Fig. 2)**. Because stitches aren't square (they are wider than they are tall), you need to apply an easing to the seam. Typically, you need to work four bars (rows) for every three stitches.

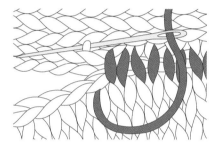

Fig. 2

Short-rows

GERMAN SHORT-ROWS

With yarn in front, sl 1 pwise from left needle to right needle. Pull yarn to back of work over needle until both legs of stitch in row below are on top of needle (as shown), creating a "double stitch" on both sides of needle **(FIG. 1)**.When working the double-stitch on subsequent rows, work both legs together as a single stitch **(FIG. 2)**.

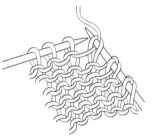

Fig. 1

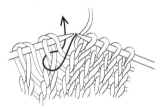

Fig. 2

WRAP & TURN SHORT-ROWS

KNIT SIDE

Work to turning point, slip next stitch purlwise **(FIG. 1)**, bring the yarn to the front, then slip the same stitch back to the left needle **(FIG. 2)**, turn the work around and bring the yarn to position for the next stitch—one stitch has been wrapped, and the yarn is correctly positioned to work the next stitch.

When you come to a wrapped stitch on a subsequent row, hide the wrap by working it together with the wrapped stitch as follows: Insert right needle tip under the wrap (from the front if wrapped stitch is a knit stitch; from the back if wrapped stitch is a purl stitch; **FIG. 3**), then into the stitch on the needle, and work the stitch and its wrap together as a single stitch.

PURL SIDE

Work to the turning point, slip the next stitch purlwise to the right needle, bring the yarn to the back of the work **(FIG. 1)**, return the slipped stitch to the left needle, bring the yarn to the front between the needles **(FIG. 2)**, and turn the work so that the knit side is facing—one stitch has been wrapped, and the yarn is correctly positioned to knit the next stitch. To hide the wrap on a subsequent purl row, work to the wrapped stitch, use the tip of the right needle to pick up the wrap from the back, place it on the left needle **(FIG. 3)**, then purl it together with the wrapped stitch.

Fig. 1

Fig. 2

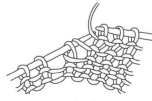

Fig. 3

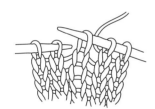

Fig. 1

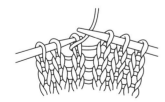

Fig. 2

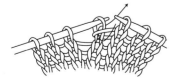

Fig. 3

APPLIED I-CORD

With double-pointed needle, cast on number of stitches directed in pattern. With right side of garment facing, *pick up and knit one stitch from edge, slide stitches to opposite end of double-pointed needle, knit to last two stitches, knit two together through the back loop; repeat from * for I-cord.

MAKING TASSELS

Cut a piece of cardboard 4" (10 cm) wide by the desired length of the tassel plus 1" (2.5 cm). Wrap yarn to desired thickness around cardboard. Cut a short length of yarn and tie tightly around one end of the wrapped yarn **(FIG. 1)**. Cut yarn loops at other end. Cut another piece of yarn and wrap tightly around loops a short distance below top knot to form tassel neck. Knot securely, thread ends onto tapestry needle, and pull to center of tassel **(FIG.2)**. Trim ends.

MAGIC LOOP

Cast on the required number of stitches. Slide them onto the cord and count off to the center of the stitches. Pinch the cord and pull it out at this point, sliding the halves of the stitches onto the actual needle bodies **(FIG. 1)**. You'll have half on one needle body, half on the other. Hold the needle that has the working yarn at the back, with the working yarn hanging at the right. Pull the back needle out, moving the live stitches to the cable. To join the round, knit the first stitch on the front needle, with the back needle, using the working yarn attached to back cable. Then continue working across the front needle **(FIG. 2)**. When you get to the end of the needle, turn your work around , slide the left needle back so that stitches are sitting on the left needle body, pull right needle out as before (moving the live stitches to the cable), and work the stitches on the other needle.

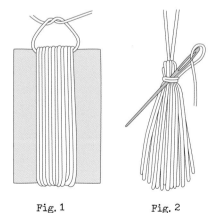

Fig. 1   Fig. 2

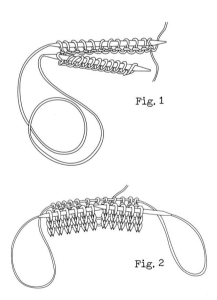

Fig. 1

Fig. 2

PICK UP AND KNIT
ALONG CO OR BO EDGE

With right side facing and working from right to left, insert the tip of the needle into the center of the stitch below the bind-off or cast-on edge **(FIG. 1)**, wrap yarn around needle, and pull through a loop **(FIG. 2)**. Pick up one stitch for every existing stitch.

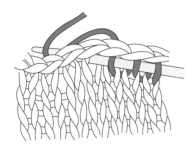

Fig. 1

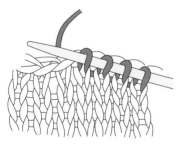

Fig. 2

POM-POM

Cut two circles of cardboard, each ½" (1.3 cm) larger than desired finished pom-pom width. Cut a small circle out of the center and a small edge out of the side of each circle **(FIG. 1)**. Tie a strand of yarn between the circles, hold circles together, and wrap with yarn—the more wraps, the thicker the pom-pom. Knot the tie strand tightly and cut between the circles **(FIG. 2)**. Place pom-pom between two smaller cardboard circles held together with a needle and trim the edges **(FIG. 3)**.

Fig. 1

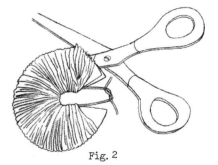

Fig. 2

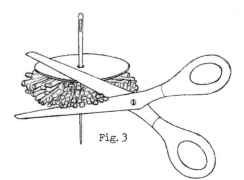

Fig. 3

ABOUT THE DESIGNERS

MEGHAN BABIN's preferred coffee is dark roast made in a French press; she usually grinds her own beans every morning and drinks an entire pot while answering morning emails. It's the only way to start the day.

HANNAH BAKER lives, knits, and sings karaoke in Fort Collins, Colorado. She is the editor of *Interweave Knits*.

KERRY BOGERT is the Editorial Director of Craft Books for F+W Media, overseeing Interweave and The Quilting Company publications. She's a Jill-of-all-crafts and finds extra satisfaction in fiber arts. She knits, crochets, spins, and weaves. Kerry has worked behind the scenes on numerous best-selling titles, including *Garter Stitch Revival*, *AlterKnit Stitch Dictionary*, *Gradient Style*, and others. You can follow her adventures in crafting on social media as @kabsconcepts.

SHANNON COOK is the designer behind the Canadian knitwear design company Very Shannon, which focuses on modern, mindful, and relaxing knits. She is continually inspired to create designs that are easy to wear and rich in texture, and that allow makers to have fun and feel confident in both her patterns and their skills.

JENNIFER DASSAU is an independent knitwear pattern designer and author of the book *Knitting Short Rows*. Find her online everywhere as knittingvortex.

MONE DRÄGER lives in a village in Germany. She loves to craft and be creative and can't imagine a day without knitting. She plays with colors and stitch patterns as she knits accessories and her favorite necessity: socks. Find out more about her crafting adventures at monemade.com.

KIRI FITZGERALD lives in Brisbane, Australia, with her husband and two children. In addition to designing, she runs and owns an online yarn shop: yayforyarn.com.au.

CATRINA FROST is an avid knitter who loves working with fiber and those who produce it. She also loves to hike with her two children and wonderful husband, who worries one day there may be sheep in the backyard.

SUE GLEAVE lives in Suffolk, United Kingdom. After a career in corporate life, she now has a second one as a dyer and knitwear designer. Her business, Native Yarns, combines her love for textiles, color, and growing things. She uses natural dyes for her yarns, some of which come from her own garden. To find out more, visit nativeyarns.co.uk.

AMY GUNDERSON lives in North Carolina with her husband and their two ornery dogs. If she's not crocheting or knitting, it's only because she's busy dog cuddling. You can find her as amygunderson on Ravelry, or cohosting the blog at universalyarn.com.

MELODY HOFFMANN is a self-taught knitter; for as long as she's been able to hold the two knitting needles, she has been obsessed. Her work is inspired and influenced by nature, minimalism, folklore, wabi-sabi and shibui, and ecology. Her designs are modern and simple but with something slightly whimsical.

EMILY KINTIGH works as an assistant in a Montessori classroom in Eugene, Oregon, which allows her to design knitting patterns in her off time. Her other designs of toys, accessories, and more can be found on Ravelry under her name.

SARA MATERNINI is the designer and founder of La Cave à Laine: modern knitting patterns and accessories for knitters. Sara is Italian and lives with her family in Alsace, France. She began to knit when she was seven, but only later in life did she transform it into a passion and then a job. She is partial to all shades of gray and blue, the right amount of pinks, and all the other colors of the world.

ANDREA RANGEL is a knitwear designer and teacher. She's the author of *AlterKnit Stitch Dictionary* and *Rugged Knits* (Interweave), and her patterns have been published in *Interweave Knits*, *knitscene*, *Brooklyn Tweed Wool People*, *Twist Collective*, and other publications, as well as independently. She lives on Vancouver Island in British Columbia.

KATHERINE ROLLINS likes to knit and write children's books. She often does both at coffee shops. You can read her musings on her blog at katherinerollins.blogspot.com.

AMY ROLLIS is a Michigan native who renewed her childhood love of knitting. Believing that every person is inherently creative, she loves the extremes of chaos and order in art and the design process, and started designing knitwear in an attempt to justify her overflowing and growing yarn stash.

KRISTEN TENDYKE designs classic sweaters with unique constructions. She specializes in seamless knitting and always keeps Mother Nature in mind when making yarn choices. Kristen strives to provide you with patterns that are easy to follow, enjoyable, and engaging to make! See more of her patterns at kristentendyke.com.

HANNAH THIESSEN is a freelance creative with a specialty in yarn and knitting-related businesses. She frequently writes and designs to communicate her deep love of wool: where and how it is made into yarn, and what it becomes in the hands of the knitter. She has dabbled in various textile-related crafts, from quilting and garment making to spinning her own yarns, knitting, and weaving. You can follow her on her website, knittingvividly.com.

CHERYL TOY is an avid knitter, instructor, and designer. After achieving a BFA in Design, Cheryl designed sets, costumes, and lighting for theater, worked for many years as an art director in film and television, and, after moving to New Orleans, was active in historical restoration. As a designer of knitwear, Cheryl has contributed to *Interweave Knits*, *knitscene*, *knit.wear*, *Love of Knitting*, *Knit Picks*, and *Creative Knitting*.

LORI WAGNER lives in Temecula, California; she learned to knit in 2008 and started self-publishing her designs in 2014. She has worked with *Interweave Knits*, *Valley Yarns*, *Knit One Crochet Too*, and *Knit Picks*. Her designs can be found on Ravelry under her name. When not obsessively knitting, she enjoys reading, hiking, or hanging out with her cats and canary!

KEEP THE INSPIRATION FLOWING WITH THESE FRESH COLLECTIONS!

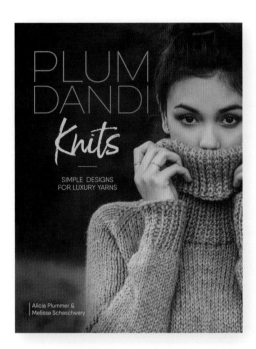

← **PLUM DANDI KNITS**

Simple Designs with Luxury Yarns

Alicia Plummer and Melissa Schaschwary

9781632505941 | $24.99

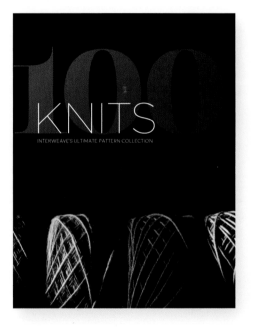

↑ **100 KNITS**

Interweave's Ultimate Pattern Collection

Interweave Editors

9781632506474 | $45.00

← **WOOL STUDIO**

The Knitwear Capsule Collection

Meghan Babin

9781632506412 | $27.99